A Woman's Guide to
Getting Through
Tough Times

> *Without wavering, let us hold tightly
> to the hope we say we have, for God
> can be trusted to keep his promise.*
>
> HEBREWS 10:23, NLT

A Woman's Guide to Getting Through Tough Times

QUIN SHERRER and RUTHANNE GARLOCK

VINE
BOOKS

SERVANT PUBLICATIONS
ANN ARBOR, MICHIGAN

Vine Books is an imprint of Servant Publications especially designed to serve evan-
gelical Christians.

Published by Servant Publications
P.O. Box 8617
Ann Arbor, Michigan 48107

Cover design and illustration: Hile Illustration & Design, Ann Arbor, MI

98 99 00 01   10 9 8 7 6 5 4 3 2 1

Printed in the United States of America
ISBN 1-56955-025-5

Library of Congress Cataloging-in-Publication Data

Sherrer, Quin.
A woman's guide to getting through tough times / Quin Sherrer and Ruthanne
Garlock.
    p.   cm.
"Vine Books."
Includes bibliographical references.
ISBN 1-56955-025-5 (alk. paper)
1. Christian women—Religious life. 2. Women—Conduct of life. I. Garlock,
Ruthanne.   II. Title.
BV4527.S427   1998
248.8'43—dc21   98-14301
                                                                 CIP

Other Books by the Authors

How to Pray for Your Children
Miracles Happen When You Pray
by Quin Sherrer

How to Forgive Your Children
How to Pray for Your Family and Friends
A Woman's Guide to Spiritual Warfare
The Spiritual Warrior's Prayer Guide
A Woman's Guide to Breaking Bondages
A Woman's Guide to Spirit-Filled Living
Prayers Women Pray
by Quin Sherrer and Ruthanne Garlock

A Christian Woman's Guide to Hospitality
by Quin Sherrer and Laura Watson

Before We Kill and Eat You
Fire in His Bones
by Ruthanne Garlock
The Christian in Complete Armour, volumes 1-3
Ruthanne Garlock was the senior editor for the abridged edition
of this Puritan classic written by William Gurnall in 1655.

Contents

Acknowledgments

I (Quin) pay tribute to my late mother whose life showed me how a single mom can maintain joy and endurance through very tough times—yet be victorious in the end:
Jewett Lammon Moore (1910–1983)

I (Ruthanne) honor two special women of faith in my life who have been wonderful examples of steadfastness through their own tough times:
Ruth Eveline Garlock (1897–1997)
My mother-in-law

Patricia Marilyn Sandidge
My sister-in-law
who stood by my brother in
his long battle with cancer
and faces the future with courage.

We also offer special thanks to:
- Our many friends and prayer partners who have faithfully prayed for and encouraged us.
- Our editors, Beth Feia and Gwen Ellis.
- All the women who allowed us to share their stories.

Introduction

THE STORY OF NOAH in the book of Genesis teaches us the importance of preparing for tough times—even when at the present moment things may seem normal. Because Noah had found favor with God, he was warned that destruction was coming. God told him how to provide safety for himself and his family.

Reflecting on the importance of being prepared for tough times, I (Ruthanne) thought about the experience my husband and I have just had in building our new home. Having never built a home before, we sought advice from knowledgeable friends and tried to take all necessary precautions. We carefully chose the most logical building site on our property, and made sure the foundation was solid.

Because during construction the area suffered the worst drought on record for fifty years, we didn't realize what would happen to our sloping front yard when rainy season rolled around. But six months after we moved in, the area then had the worst *flooding* on record for fifty years! And it came in June, a time when normally there is very little rain.

My husband was out of the country at the time, and I was gone during the weekend the storm hit. I came home to find mud on our porch almost all the way up to the front door. I was grateful no water had gotten into the house—though many people in the area suffered tremendous flood damage. The slope in front of the house hadn't seemed so steep in dry weather. But with torrential rain, it becomes a waterfall. The out-of-season rain was a warning that we needed to take preventive measures.

Now, as the fall rainy season is under way, we've just finished building a retaining wall across the front yard that will divert rainwater to either side of the property and protect the house from any future flooding. We learned our lesson. We now stand prepared.

The spiritual analogy seems clear. God, in his grace, warns us, and gives a window of time in which to prepare for coming storms. If we respond, doing what we can with our limited understanding, he provides the necessary strength and wisdom to build a protective wall. God is an ally in tough times.

By contrast, the false gods worshiped by millions of people in our world seem to be enemies. Driven by fear that evil spirits may harm them or their families, the "worshippers" strive to appease these gods through their rituals.

A missionary working in Asia recently told me of one of her students who had broken with traditions to embrace faith in Christ. He is suffering tremendous persecution at the hands of his own family, but at last he has inner peace. Knowing his Creator-God is a redemptive, loving Father enables him to endure tough times.

What a contrast to the truth that our Creator-God is a redemptive, loving Father. Though we're not guaranteed sunny skies and smooth sailing, neither does God purposely seek vengeance against his children. He offers grace and forgiveness for our sins, and promises his presence and his peace to sustain us through the storm.

Over my kitchen window hangs a plaque with a picture of an ark, a rainbow, and a dove, with the inscription *God Keeps His Promises*. It's a constant reminder that, even when I'm going through tough times, God is faithful to his Word.

—Ruthanne Garlock

ONE

Are You Going Through Tough Times?

Dear friends, do not be surprised at the painful trial you are suffering, as though something strange were happening to you. But rejoice that you participate in the sufferings of Christ, so that you may be overjoyed when his glory is revealed.

1 PETER 4:12–13

Why did Christ keep His scars? He could have had a perfect body, or no body, when He returned to splendor in heaven. Instead He carried with Him remembrances of His visit to earth. For a reminder of His time here, He chose scars. That is why I say God hears and understands our pain, and even absorbs it into Himself—because He kept those scars as a lasting image of wounded humanity. He has been here; He has borne the sentence. The pain of man has become the pain of God.[1]

DR. PAUL BRAND

*T*ough times. Troubles and trials. We've all had them, but how many of us have delighted in the experience? Instead we pray they will pass, and soon. Seldom do we rejoice over tough times—we're more likely to blame them on the devil. Or on God.

But the truth is, severe adversity does come—often to those who we believe deserve it least. And the speedy deliverance we hope and pray for doesn't always follow.

If you are struggling to get through a difficult period in your life, you're one of a very large company of God's people. Not only of this present time, but of the biblical company that includes Joseph and his unjust treatment ... Hannah and her travail for a child ... David and his fear of Saul ... Daniel, who was persecuted for praying ... the woman at the well, who'd been rejected by five successive husbands. The apostle Paul, who suffered shipwreck, beatings, and imprisonment, wrote, "All these things happened to them as examples, and they were written for our admonition" (1 Cor 10:11, NKJ).

The Helmet of Hope

For many years now, we have been writing and teaching on spiritual warfare—encouraging believers to use their spiritual weapons and take a stand against Satan's attacks. Occasionally we encounter women who get the mistaken idea that spiritual warfare is a quick and easy solution to their difficulties. Then they are disappointed when the battle persists, and principles they've learned seem not to work.

We definitely affirm the validity of spiritual warfare. But we also recognize that some battles are intense and long-term, demanding great tenacity and commitment before the problem is resolved.

An essential piece of armor we're to wear in the midst of battle is the helmet of salvation and hope (see Eph 6:17 and 1 Thes 5:8). Author Roger Palms shares this analogy: "When you have salvation, not as a wispy kerchief but as a firm, hard reality, and you have it on when you face life, then no unexpected explosions, no sudden blows, can topple you.... Think of life as a hard-hat area. Think of the hope of salvation as a helmet. It will change your perspective on how you face each day and the events in it."[2]

The purpose of this book is to provide guidelines to *help* you get through your valley of tough times. Also to offer *hope*—assuring you that you can come out of the experience wiser, better, and stronger than when you went into it. And to urge you to receive God's *healing* for the hurts you've acquired along the way.

You will meet women who have survived difficulties similar to yours, and others whose trials may make yours seem like a "light affliction" by comparison. The insights these friends share from their experiences will encourage and strengthen you to persevere no matter what the trial.

Both of us have dealt with our share of tough times over the years. One of Quin's greatest challenges was overcoming the hurts of her childhood. She shares here a final chapter in her healing, which took place while we were writing this book.

A Painful Journey

More than forty years had passed since my last visit to this huge old stone building in the Texas hill country. Back then it had been converted from a skating rink into an assembly hall for a denominational youth camp. Today it's part of a retreat center.

As Ruthanne and I stood in a corner of the room, a patch of sunlight filtered through the window and my thoughts rushed back to the only other time I had stood here. For a shy fifteen-year-old who didn't know a single person at the youth camp, the experience I am about to relate was all the more frightening.

It was my first trip back to Texas to visit my father after he had abandoned my mother and us four children three years earlier. When I'd written Mom that I wanted to come back to Florida because I was uncomfortable at his home where a new wife resided, she wired him to send me back to her.

Instead, he sent me to the youth camp, but it proved to be his undoing. Daddy was a pastor, and some of the denominational leaders at the camp recognized me as his oldest child. They took me aside to this same corner of the assembly hall to interrogate me about the details of my parents' breakup.

I was miserable and embarrassed being on the firing line, but I gave honest answers. As their probing questions went on, the truth of what had happened unfolded. Daddy had moved his secretary in with us, then after sending us away, married her. A few months following that interrogation, those same leaders asked him to resign his pastorate. Because he had several degrees, he managed to keep a teaching job, but as far as I know he never preached again.

Several years passed before I next saw Daddy, but whenever I thought of that ranch in the hills of Texas, bad feelings and memories swept over me. A sense of remorse that this brilliant man's preaching career had ended. Perhaps a sense of guilt that I'd caused it. Regret that because he cut himself off from us, our family suffered financial hardship as Mom struggled to support four children in an old clapboard boarding house, determined to see us all through college.

I had been hurt not only by his abandonment; the double standard he had displayed gave me a negative view of God as Father. Gifted in preaching, Daddy was a favorite speaker for big denominational events, but at home he was a hard taskmaster. He expected perfection from his children—from demanding absolute quiet while he napped, to pressuring us to make all A's in school. He was quick to punish my brothers with a leather belt, but rarely expressed any affection or approval to any of us.

Shy and quiet, I studied all the time to avoid his anger. But I would wonder, *Do I have to try as hard to earn God's approval as I do Daddy's? Will God see me as "less than" if I bring home a B instead of an A? Or if I haven't memorized all the required Bible verses? Or if I were actually to go to a movie with a friend?*

I remember the sense of shame I felt as the only one in my class who came from a divorced home. I was even turned down for church membership because of it in the very denomination that had ordained my father—as if the breakup were my fault. My understanding of Father God, as well as my attitude toward pastors, became distorted.

Bringing Closure

So here we stood, Ruthanne and I, in the same corner where I'd undergone "the inquisition" years before. All I could do was ask God to complete the healing of hurts I had suffered here, even though Daddy had been dead several years now.

While standing there, memories filled my mind of another time—a night in 1972—when I had chosen to forgive my father while a pastor I didn't even know prayed with me. I had wept tears of repentance as the Holy Spirit swept away all the buried feelings of anger, rejection, unforgiveness, and bitterness that I'd carried for so long. That night I saw a clearer picture of a loving heavenly Father, and was able to forgive pastors in general for what I felt were injustices. I even began writing to Daddy and developing a long-distance relationship.

Then I remembered another day a few years after that important prayer. It was the second time my dad ever came to see me. "I'm so glad you have forgiven me," he said as he was leaving. I was able to hug him and mean it when I whispered, "It's all right, Daddy."

Now, as Ruthanne and I turned to leave, a maintenance man entered the room to sweep up. Walking out, we passed bags of garbage and an overflowing trash can waiting to be carted off. For me, final closure to a long period of pain and struggle in my life came when I went back to that old building and turned over to the Lord any leftover emotional garbage.

We left the assembly hall and drove up to an outdoor chapel on the highest hill overlooking the retreat center. There we exulted over the gorgeous view of God's creation and had a praise celebration for the ending of that pain in my life. As we drove out of the gates of the compound I could truly say I was glad I had come. During the drive back to Ruthanne's new home only seventy miles away, we talked about the many women we'd prayed with over the years who had suffered great emotional pain because of similar experiences.

We exercise some control over just how long our sojourn in the valley of tough times will continue. Only when we choose to forgive the person who caused the pain can the healing process begin. The Holy Spirit is always available to strengthen and help us once we make the choice to forgive.

Closure may come when you write your feelings and confession to the Lord in a journal, or "pray through" on the matter with a prayer partner. You may need to visit or write those involved in the painful situation to let them know you've forgiven them. Or perhaps you will be led to go to a site where a significant event took place and release those memories to the Lord. But be assured, if you want to receive God's healing, the Holy Spirit will guide you and help you when you choose to forgive.

Vignettes of Tough Times

Perhaps you can identify with some of these tough-times scenarios women have shared with us:

- A grandmother who is raising her year-old twin grandsons after her daughter abandoned them.
- A wife who is struggling in her marriage because her husband is addicted to pornography.
- A nurse working in a hospital for emotionally disturbed children who is falsely accused of abusing one of the patients. The charge is initiated by a coworker who is jealous of her position.
- A couple almost ready for retirement who are now having to put their adult daughter into a drug rehab program and take care of her toddler.
- A mother who must coach her learning-disabled son through everything twice—repeating classes, going to summer school every year, with no end in sight.
- A mother who accompanied her daughter to get an abortion and now suffers with guilt over agreeing to the death of what would have been her first grandchild. Though she has asked God's forgiveness, she finds it hard to forgive herself.
- A mother whose son was killed in an auto accident and who now wrestles with God about whether it was he or Satan who took the boy's life.

- A young woman who grew up in a home with an alcoholic father and now struggles with anger because he committed suicide—after the whole family had worked very hard to help him and to keep things stable for him.

- A woman whose estranged daughter finally calls her after four years because she's desperate for money. During the time the daughter had remained out of contact with her family, she had suffered eating disorders and attacks of depression, and had attempted suicide.

- A young woman who still grieves several years after her fiancé canceled their wedding only two weeks before the ceremony.

Hurting Is Real

Normal transitions in our lives, such as job losses, relocations, or children marrying and moving away, can bring hurting times. But the more traumatic challenges stretch us even more and cause us to change our perspective on what is truly important. In her book *The Pummeled Heart,* Antoinette Bosco gives important insights from her own years of suffering:

Imagine, for example, if your child is in danger of death— and I have lost two sons—how little such things as furniture, a clean house, a job promotion, or a cranky relative matter. You become terribly conscious of how finite this world is and you reach out for what is lasting, the Eternal. You go to God.

... Another pitfall that can threaten us is what I bluntly call the periodic, temporary loss of faith. We get overcome with the dark feeling that nothing makes sense. It is a bleak place to be. But we find ourselves there now and then simply because that's life.... What has astounded me in such times is how remarkably and surprisingly God re-reveals his creative power to help us hang on to faith.[3]

A Mother's Legacy of Grace

I (Quin) came to know God's peace in the dark days of caring for my mother during the thirteen months she suffered with cancer. When she was in agony because the pain medication gave no relief, my son Keith would sometimes sit beside her bed, slamming his fist into his palm, and cry, "Why? Why must Mother Jewett suffer so?"

My only explanation came from two verses that had become precious to me and to Mom: "That I may know Him and the power of His resurrection, and the fellowship of His sufferings" (Phil 3:10, NKJV). "If we died with Him, we shall also live with Him; if we endure, we shall also reign with Him" (2 Tm 2:11-12, NKJV).

It was small comfort to my twenty-one-year-old son, but to my dying seventy-two-year-old mother, it was hope.

Toward the end of her very tough journey, she asked me to bring her a pen and tablet so she could write one last letter to her children. Despite her weakness, she labored for hours to write this from her bed at home. It is a legacy I treasure:

My dear children,

Before I took off on a trip, I used to have a real urgency to write to each of you. Now I feel that urgency again.

As each of you know, I've been very independent and felt I could handle any situation that came my way. This struggle of coping with cancer is truly a learning experience. At first decisions had to be made—picking the right doctor, treatment, handling legal matters—which along with the shock, pain, and suffering were most difficult.

I know I had the support of each of you four children along with family and a host of friends. But I needed God's grace to see me through. I've learned so much through this. One of the hard things about suffering is that when others learn you are suffering, they get involved and suffer too. I know Jesus' purpose in suffering on the cross was to bring us to God. He suffered for us.

The other night I said, "Lord, give me grace to endure. I want this to be an opportunity, not an ordeal. I don't want to have any bad feelings or any murmurings."

It was as if big floodgates instantly opened. The grace and love of God flooded my being. It was the most marvelous experience, and everything changed in me. I never felt the love for each of you children so much. Since then I've felt the joy of the Lord and His grace, and know that peace which passes all understanding will sustain and carry me through.

So to each of you, I trust this will be an opportunity and not an ordeal. I desire you to know God's grace is sufficient for you.

My future is in God's hands, and whatever the need, it will be met when that time arrives.

All my love, Mother

Three months later, just two days after Easter, she slipped away to her heavenly home. After her funeral service, I led the family's processional behind her casket as we and the whole congregation in that little Episcopal church sang, "Christ the Lord is risen today, Hallelujah!" The funeral director didn't want to go to the cemetery because it was raining so hard, but I insisted that we go for the final grave-side service. Just as we got there, the rain stopped, the clouds parted, and we said our last good-byes as we committed Mom to her heavenly Father. Then the heavens opened up and spilled their tears again.

I hope when my toughest time on earth comes, I can say with Mom, "Lord, give me grace to endure. I want this to be an opportunity, not an ordeal."

The Bible says there is a time to be born and a time to die (see Eccl 3:2). Each one of us will face death someday. Can we, will we, be ready to meet our Lord, with no regrets?

God's Embroidery

A poem the Dutch evangelist Corrie ten Boom often used in her teaching is about a piece of embroidery. While displaying a piece of needlework, she would say, "God knows what we do not know. God knows all. Look at this piece of embroidery. The wrong side is chaos. But look at the beautiful picture on the other side—the right side." Then she would repeat this poem:

My life is but a weaving, between my Lord and me,
I cannot choose the colors, He weaveth steadily.
Ofttimes He weaveth sorrow, and I in foolish pride
Forget He sees the upper, and I, the underside.
Not 'til the loom is silent and the shuttles cease to fly,
Shall God unroll the canvas and explain the reason why.
The dark threads are as needful in the skillful Weaver's
    hand
As the threads of gold and silver in the pattern He has
    planned.

"We see now the wrong side; God sees his side all the time," Corrie would add. "One day we shall see the embroidery from his side, and thank him for every answered and unanswered prayer. The joyful thing is that all the time we have to fight the fight of faith, God sees his side of the embroidery. God has no problems concerning our lives—only plans. There is no panic in heaven."[4]

Prayer

Lord, I admit I don't like tough times, troubles, and tribulation. Rejoicing in the midst of my trial is not easy; I need your strength. Help me to praise you in spite of the circumstances, and to hang on in faith that this situation will eventually pass. Lord, I want to emerge better and more Christlike—not bitter and resentful. Help me to reflect your glory in my attitude, my behavior, and my character. Thank you, Lord Jesus, for suffering for me. Amen.

TWO

When Hardship Hits Home

Therefore we do not lose heart. Though outwardly we are wasting away, yet inwardly we are being renewed day by day. For our light and momentary troubles are achieving for us an eternal glory that far outweighs them all. So we fix our eyes not on what is seen, but on what is unseen. For what is seen is temporary, but what is unseen is eternal.

2 CORINTHIANS 4:16-18

I can see that Jesus drew men and women into the Kingdom by promising them two things: first, trouble—hardship, danger; and second, joy. But what curious alchemy is this that He can make even danger and hardship seem joyous? He understands things about human nature that we grasp only dimly: few of us are really challenged by the promise of soft living, by an emphasis on me-first, or by a life of easy compromise.[1]

CATHERINE MARSHALL

"Why? Why did this happen to me? And why now? What did I do to deserve this suffering?" Have you ever asked God those questions? Probably most of us have thought them, even if we didn't speak them. Another question we could ask is, "Why not me? Why should I be spared pain and suffering any more than anyone else?"

Making a Choice

None of us escapes adversity in this life. But we do have a choice: either to allow God's grace to test our hearts, then change us in the midst of our suffering; or to harden our hearts in bitterness.

Whatever pain we suffer, or whatever loss we experience in our adversity, God will use it for good. Scripture provides many accounts of God's people braving hardship—for example, when the Israelites were delivered from slavery in Egypt, followed by the forty years of wilderness wanderings. Their own disobedience was responsible for much of the suffering they endured. But God, instead of destroying them, reminded them he was developing their character: "Remember how the Lord your God led you all the way in the desert these forty years, to humble you and to test you in order to know what was in your heart, whether or not you would keep his commands" (Dt 8:2).

When troubles press in, we scarcely see how God could be developing our character. We just want the trial to be over.

But testing does reveal the depth of our trust in God, as well as our shallow places of doubt and fear.

A Wilderness Road

The wilderness experience for Helen took her down a road she never dreamed she'd have to walk. "Drama and trauma seem to have become my companions since I became a single parent," she told us. "Sometimes I wonder how it would feel not to be dealing with a crisis."

After years of praying for her husband's salvation, his hardness toward God and toward her only increased. His cruel verbal and emotional abuse caused their oldest daughter, Lisa, to require psychiatric counseling in her early teen years.

"I realized then I had to file for divorce to protect my children," Helen said. "I agonized over whether my trying to stay in the marriage had caused more suffering for the kids. But God sustained me through the hassles of the divorce, helping me with employment and getting counseling help for Lisa. It wasn't easy, but I grew a lot in the experience."

Helen felt that once her kids finished high school, then settled into college or a job, life would become a bit easier. But nothing prepared her for the next ordeal she was about to encounter. She tells her story:

"The summer after Lisa's first year of nurse's training, I noticed she was spending a lot of time alone with Kenny, her first serious boyfriend. I warned her to use boundaries and not to put herself in compromising situations. We'd had many open discussions about sexual matters. She and Kenny, both believers, had met at church and dated steadily for several months.

"Toward the end of that summer she came to me in tears, confessing that she'd had sex with Kenny. We had a sober, tender, firm discussion late into the night. 'Lisa, let this be God's hand of mercy to you—don't do it again!' I said. She assured me she would not, and I trusted her. I felt she would now walk in a healthy fear of the Lord.

"But two months later while we were out driving one evening, Lisa announced other news: 'Mom, my life will change forever. I'm pregnant. I've tested positive on two tests.' She had had sex with Kenny two more times after her repentance and our discussion.

"'We're going to Kenny's place,' I said grimly, turning the car around to head toward his apartment.

"I confronted both of them about their wrongdoing and held them accountable for their actions as I expressed my deep concern, hurt, and disappointment. God helped me to stay calm during the entire discussion; then afterward a surge of anger and violence swept over me.

"Of course I was angry with Lisa, but I really wanted to hurt Kenny. He is a few years older than Lisa, and I felt he took advantage of an inexperienced teenager. I wanted to jam the phone into his stomach, step on his toes, and generally beat him up.

"I was devastated and filled with shame, as it seemed my best efforts at child-rearing had failed. With a dark cloud now hanging over Lisa's promising future, I felt disappointment, anger, hurt, grief, and loss with this news. Then I entered a three-month period of depression. Although I never turned my back on God, I felt numb and lifeless, not caring about anything anymore.

"Meanwhile, Lisa suffered extreme morning sickness as she entered her second year of nursing school. She and Kenny struggled over whether to get married, or to give up the baby for adoption. Much of the time it seemed to me like a bad dream I hoped would soon be over.

"One day, almost three months after Lisa's announcement, I was sitting alone at the kitchen table. In the spirit, I felt and saw the Lord come into the room. Like a good friend would do, he gently slapped me on the shoulder and said reassuringly, 'Don't you think my love is big enough to cover this situation?'

"That moment was the turning point for me in this journey. I suddenly saw the whole problem from God's perspective—that it wasn't hopeless. Now I could accept Lisa more freely and receive Kenny as a son. I repented for my anger, forgave both of them for disappointing me, and moved out of the holding pattern to get on with my life.

"After finishing her second year of study, Lisa delivered a healthy little boy. She and Kenny are now married and she is taking her third year of training. Their wedding was a testimony of God's healing, with the baby and all family members present.

"After repeating their vows to each other, they had the pastor dedicate their son. It was a spiritual experience of restoration, declaring to the seen and unseen world that God forgives, heals, delivers, and redeems our mistakes.

"The drama of the pregnancy, and the trauma of becoming a grandmother before becoming a mother-in-law, almost overwhelmed me. I could deal with these events only by keeping my focus on Jesus, blocking out quiet times in my schedule to seek his presence, and letting go of the things over which I had no control.

"Now the hardest thing is to see Lisa going through 'adjustment-to-life' pains, as the changes have come so fast for both of us. I know she has more hard lessons still ahead of her, but she's certainly older and wiser after this experience. I'm learning to trust God to show me when to step back and let her grow, and when to step toward her to encourage and reinforce. These life lessons are still in process, but my faith is anchored in knowing his love truly is big enough for every situation."

Creating a Blended Family

In our book *A Woman's Guide to Spiritual Warfare,* we shared the story of Rena, whose marriage failed despite her prayers and efforts to salvage it. She struggled to comfort her two disappointed sons, while also adjusting to a new location and a new job teaching music. Then she met Trent, a single father struggling to raise his two sons alone after his wife had walked out. Soon he proposed marriage.

Rena was very cautious, but after three years of prayer and

counseling, they were married. Although her divorce had been painful, Rena discovered creating a blended family in crowded quarters brought hardship, too. The personalities of her sons and Trent's sons were poles apart, and learning to trust "outsiders" wasn't easy. Setting guidelines for discipline and household routines brought flashes of conflict.

"The Lord began dealing with me about my own attitudes, and through a lot of tears I called on him to help me love with his love," Rena said. "Solutions came slowly. But I learned to depend on Trent to handle discipline issues, and concentrate on being a loving care-giver. In spite of my teaching schedule, I try to prepare at least one good, hot meal a day which all six of us share together as a family. That alone has brought down a lot of walls."

Now, after four years, Rena rejoices in the spiritual breakthroughs she and Trent are beginning to see in their boys.

"Trent's steadfastness has helped my sons learn to trust again," Rena said. "In fact, all the boys now refer to one another as brothers. They pray for one another, and they have a common interest in music. As they're being healed of their own hurts, they're able to overcome selfishness and reach out to others.

"God has brought us a long way toward being a family blended by love. In coping with the tough times, I always find renewal and strength through worship. The piano is my place of prayer, warfare, and refuge where I express my feelings to the Lord and receive his love and peace."

Holding on to God

When financial hardship hits, coupled with losing your home and livelihood, the worry and pressure can easily overshadow your confidence in God. Getting through such a time calls for a determination to hold on to your trust in Father God. Ruth, once a farmer's wife, wrote us about her trauma in going through financial loss:

"In the 1980s we found ourselves in debt to the bank because of farm-operation loans that we could not repay. The bank had encouraged expansion and development, but within a short time farm prices and the cattle market plunged. This meant foreclosure, bankruptcy, and selling off our possessions.

"We had purchased the homeplace from my husband's parents, and the pastureland from my grandparents— property that had been in the family for generations. We felt a great responsibility to carry on that heritage.

"However, we had to sell the cattle, then were no longer ranchers. We auctioned off the machinery and were no longer farmers. Next was the land. With that finally gone, we not only suffered great financial loss; we lost what our parents and grandparents had worked so hard to keep. We went from a net worth of one million dollars to zero.

"One day, looking at the farm machinery all lined up for the sale, I remembered what a friend had said when their tractor had fallen apart: 'Big deal—it's just a piece of steel.' I put a sign on the chicken house that read, 'There is life after farming!' My only recourse was to hold on to my faith in God—that was something they couldn't take from me.

"We moved to a rented house in a nearby town and my husband started a new business. We received a small donation from a farm-relief benefit that helped us buy groceries. Many friends sent money anonymously through the mail.

"But ten years later—after losing the farm, living in a rented home, then moving in with relatives because of business failures—I found myself facing a divorce. Our thirty-five-year marriage didn't survive the strain of all our losses. Yet the Lord has proved himself faithful over and over as my provider and husband, and he continues to uphold me.

"I do not understand all that has happened to me, or why it has happened. But I do understand that this earth is not my real home. Jesus lives within me, and I will dwell in his house forever, where he has prepared a place for me.

"My rope of hope is this verse: "'For I know the plans I have for you," declares the Lord, "plans to prosper you and not to harm you, plans to give you hope and a future. Then you will call upon me and come and pray to me, and I will listen to you…. I will bring you back from captivity…"'" (Jer 29:11-12, 14a).

Tough Times Early in Life

Losses in life generally defy our understanding—especially the death of a loved one. It seems so dreadful, so final. But by making the loss less fearful, a young girl's mother left her daughter with a legacy of putting her trust in God.

JoNell was twelve years old when her father died on a Tuesday and was buried two days later. On Friday morning her mother said, "Jo Baby, it will be hard, but you'll have to go back to school today. We have to get back to living. We've got to trust this was God's will for your daddy. As hard as it is on us, God will be faithful."

It was her first time to deal with death or tragedy. But the way her mom helped the family get back to living was a lesson that stuck with JoNell and has helped her through many tough times since.

"From then on, I was convinced nothing passes God's attention," JoNell said. "Even though we don't understand some situations, God is faithful—just like Mama told me. Though I was twelve, I could still crawl up on Daddy's lap and know he was my protector. After he died I missed him terribly, and many times longed to have him hold me again and comfort me. But when Mom assured me that our heavenly Father loved me more than my earthly father, I knew I'd never have to worry about God's trustworthiness. I could crawl up on his lap, too.

"After Daddy died, I stayed home with Mama until I married at twenty. Over the years I watched her trust God for everything. She taught me about God's character without even realizing it. The other traumas I experienced after that were easier to go through because of the life lesson I'd learned from her: 'As hard as it is on us, God will be faithful.'"

Overcoming Fear

Because we're often traumatized by fear when we suffer loss and hardship, we struggle to keep our focus on the Lord and to draw strength from him. Devotional writer Hannah Whitall Smith offers this antidote to fear:

> A large part of the pain of life comes from the haunting "fear of evil" which so often besets us. Our lives are full of supposes. Suppose this should happen, or suppose that should happen; what could we do; how could we bear it? But, if we are living in the "high tower" of the dwelling place of God, all these supposes will drop out of our lives. We shall be "quiet from the fear of evil," for no threatenings of evil can penetrate into the "high tower" of God. Even when walking through the valley of the shadow of death, the psalmist could say, "I will fear no evil"; and, if we are dwelling in God, we can say so too.[2]

No Surprises With God

Fear and doubt crowded Millie's mind as she and her husband drove south in a rented motor home to pick up her recently widowed father-in-law and his retarded adult son, Donnie. Millie's children were grown, and she was the only "stay at home" wife in the family available to serve as caregiver.

Just two days earlier they had agreed they would make room in their home for Grandpa and Donnie, but she'd had little time to prepare.

On the road, as Millie began to agonize about the uncertainties that lay ahead, she kept playing a tape of this song: *Whatever my lot, Thou hast taught me to say, It is well, it is well with my soul....* And somehow she knew God would carry her through.

"I was totally unprepared for Donnie when he first came to live with us," Millie said. "But when he realized he could call me 'Ma' and that I did for him all the things his mother had done, he began to adjust. I learned to take him with me wherever I went, just as if he were a child. I had to watch him so he wouldn't get lost, remind him to use the bathroom and wash his hands, and repeatedly urge him, 'Don't pick your nose.'"

Even after Grandpa died, Donnie stayed on with Millie and her husband. For ten years now she has been substitute mom to Donnie, a fifty-seven-year-old with the behavior of a three-to five-year-old child.

"It's not always easy living with a perpetual child—especially when he goes through stubborn, angry, noncompliant phases when he won't eat or get out of bed. We call them 'alligator days.' But we've learned to deal with whatever comes, and I'm careful not to think of the 'what ifs.' My life is full of love and is enriched by having Donnie.

"God doesn't allow us to choose the cross he expects us to pick up daily and carry," Millie says. "First he arranges our circumstances, and then he supplies the grace and help we need to do what he has set before us to do."

Evelyn Christenson emphasizes the importance of turning things over to our all-wise Father:

We may pray for something that seems very good to us, but God knows the "what ifs" in our lives. He knows the calamities that might occur if He answered our prayers in the way we think best. He also knows about all our difficult situations and wants to turn them into something tremendously good.

... Maybe we'll have to get to heaven before we understand some things, but it's exciting to recognize as the years come and go that everything has worked together for good if we have really loved Him.

... When we pray for answers, we're demanding that God do something and telling Him we want it done now—"just the way we want it, Lord." When we're bringing our requests to Him, we're saying, "Lord, here's the need" ... then we ask Him to answer according to His omniscient will.[3]

Seeing the Invisible

If ever a woman had a "right" to be bitter, Fanny Crosby did. Blinded as an infant because of a doctor's inept treatment, she grew up in poverty without a father, and at age fourteen had to leave home to get an education. While teaching at an institute for the blind, she married one of her colleagues.

Fanny found happiness living with her husband in a small

village, where she took care of her baby and wrote poetry. But when the baby died and she and her husband moved back to a shabby New York apartment, her grief pushed her almost to despair. The marriage eventually ended in separation, and her poetry writing and charity work for the church could not fill the void in her life.

Then a pastor introduced her to a musician who needed someone to write lyrics for the music he composed. They formed a partnership, and Fanny knew she'd found her life's work. She never blamed God for her blindness; instead she felt he helped her turn her pain into poetry and song.

One account says of her:

She was doing what she loved—listening for heaven's music and putting it into everyday words that common people could sing.

... Her best loved songs were translated into many languages and still grace the pages of most church hymnals. For the past one hundred years people have been won to Christ, strengthened, and comforted by singing such favorites as "God Will Take Care of You," "Blessed Assurance," "I Am Thine, O Lord," "Jesus, Keep Me Near the Cross," and "Pass Me Not, O Gentle Savior." Rather than destroying her life, Fanny's blindness shut out enough of the world so she could hear the music of heaven. She said, "Sightless, I see, and, seeing, find soul-vision, though my eyes are blind." That vision strengthened her to work until the age of ninety-one.[4]

Help for the Wilderness

We can respond to hardship in various ways, but Dean Sherman suggests these guidelines for what to do when you're going through a wilderness:

- Truly thank the Lord for showing you the things in your heart.

- Repent, asking God to forgive any sin or wrong motives. You may also need to ask others to forgive you.

- Seek God's help to overcome and create new habits and attitudes.

- Resist the enemy in his attempts in your life.

- Never deny that you are going through a wilderness experience.

- Never feel condemned for that which has surfaced during your wilderness experience.

- Simply say, "Thank you, God, for showing me what was in my heart. Now I'll do something about it."[5]

Prayer

Lord, you see the hardship I'm struggling with right now. It's painful. Please give me your peace in the midst of this testing. Reveal what is in my heart, and help me to deal with it. Then renew my mind to see this hardship from your perspective.

I repent for not having a grateful heart. Lord, forgive me for mumbling and complaining about your provision in the desert—just as the Israelites did. My situation could be so much worse. Thank you, Father, for all that your hand has provided. I'm trusting you to take me through this trial to victory. Amen.

THREE

Healing Family Heartaches

*When you pass through the waters, I will be with you; and
when you walk through the fire, you will not be burned;
the flames will not set you ablaze. For I am the Lord, your
God, the Holy One of Israel; your Savior.*

ISAIAH 43:2-3

You are standing in a stream with water rushing around
your ankles. The waters that pass you by at that
moment, you will never see again. So it is with the misery that has challenged your life. Let it go, let it rush on
by.... There is something about going through dilem-
mas and crises that lets us discover things about God
which we would not have known under any other circumstances.[1]

T.D. JAKES

*W*hat image comes to mind when you hear the word *family?* For some it's a photo album filled with happy memories and smiling faces from childhood—a father, mother, and siblings, as well as grandparents, aunts, uncles, and cousins—enjoying special times together.

For others the word *family* brings thoughts of rejection, disappointment, abandonment, pain, or abuse—a flood of negative emotions. But whether good, bad, or indifferent, your family is the likeliest primary influence that shapes the sort of person you become.

We find some of our greatest joys in family relationships. In times of hardship or loss, their loving support provides strength and comfort. But, conversely, some of the deepest trials we ever experience concern crises with our family members, or pertain to conflict within the family. God's dealings with mankind seem always to be in the context of family. He sent Jesus to earth to become one of us and experience suffering so we could have the opportunity to be reconciled to our heavenly Father. "Since he himself has now been through suffering and temptation, he knows what it is like when we suffer and are tempted, and he is wonderfully able to help us" (Heb 2:18, TLB).

Learning to Trust God

"Lord, I'll be grateful for whatever you give, but I would love to have a little girl," Myrna prayed while looking forward to the birth of her second child. As she continued praying throughout the pregnancy, she felt one day the Lord spoke a promise to her: "This baby will be an answer to prayer." She took that to mean she would have a healthy little girl, just as she had hoped. She had no idea of the suffering that lay ahead of her. Melinda was born with normal birth weight and good color, and there were no difficulties in the delivery. But Myrna and her husband, Charles, saw their beautiful little girl only briefly, then were left waiting in the birthing room for six hours. When Myrna asked the nurses to bring her the baby, she got evasive answers that left her wondering what had happened.

Finally a doctor came in and explained that twenty minutes after her birth, Melinda had stopped breathing. A nurse happened to notice the baby turning blue and took immediate action to get her breathing again. Because the baby had had a seizure, they knew some degree of brain damage had occurred during those few seconds. She would have to stay in intensive care for observation and treatment. Had the nurse not seen the problem, Melinda probably would have been another crib death statistic, he said.

Myrna could hardly believe the doctor was talking about her baby, who had looked so normal and healthy at birth. She and Charles immediately began crying out to God for their baby's healing. After two weeks the doctors released Melinda from the hospital with their diagnosis: a mild case of cerebral palsy with epileptic tendencies.

"A nurse came to teach me how to give medication on a very strict schedule to prevent Melinda from having more seizures," Myrna said. "Afraid she might stop breathing again, I stayed up all night the first two nights to watch her, and couldn't talk to anyone without crying. The third night Charles finally said, 'Honey, we're just going to have to trust God to take care of Melinda.' Prayer became the mainstay of my life as I looked to God to help me care for this baby."

Because of the antiseizure medication, Melinda was very slow to develop in several areas. It seemed all she did was laugh and sleep—almost like a drug addict.

"As long as she was drugged like that, I felt there was no hope of her developing to her greatest potential," Myrna shared. "The doctor reluctantly agreed to wean her off the medication, saying if Melinda had any seizures they would put her back on it and increase the dosage. But once she was weaned, her development improved. I began praising God for every small bit of progress she made."

Because her left side was affected by the brain damage, Melinda needed braces to help her learn to walk. In answer to prayer, Myrna found a Jewish preschool facility for handicapped children. By age three, Melinda was walking. Then came the challenge of where to enroll her in school.

"She had to be thoroughly tested before they would accept her in public school," Myrna reported. "We prayed she would pass. The Lord had told me this child would be an answer to prayer—and literally every step of her life has been just that. She passed every one of the tests."

At age five, Melinda had a seizure at school one day, followed a few weeks later by a frightening twenty-minute seizure in the car one afternoon. They had no choice but to start medicating her again. Her vision problems made her prone to tripping and falling, so at age eight she had surgery on her left eye to straighten it. She kept getting stronger and able to do more things for herself.

"Melinda is now twelve, hasn't had another seizure, and her dosage is only a fourth of what it was before," Myrna said. "She'll soon be off that medicine altogether. But she has Attention Deficit Disorder, and the medication she takes for that suppresses her appetite. So I'm constantly trying to get her to eat and keep her at a normal weight. We've also had to deal with her having nightmares, but through prayer they've disappeared.

"Every evening I spend several hours helping her with homework, and as her grade level increases it gets harder for her. She's in seventh grade now and has never had to be held back because she couldn't keep up. She's two years behind in her learning capacity, but when she's with other kids her age, she outshines them because of her self-assurance and social skills."

Sometimes when Melinda gets discouraged, Myrna tells her, "Melinda, we have to pray. When you're struggling, just try to focus on the Lord and ask him to help you." Then they pray and worship the Lord together—and Melinda is ready to go on. When Myrna tells her she always has the choice to go into special education to make things easier, she says, "No, Mom, I want to try a little harder."

In reflecting on her walk with the Lord, Myrna realizes these difficult years have greatly strengthened her prayer life and increased her faith.

"When I first accepted the Lord before I was married, I

remember asking God to make me a woman of great faith," she said. "I had no idea what it would mean for that prayer to be answered. I want to shout from the housetops, giving thanks to the Lord for all he has done."

"We're in This Together"

Many people consider having a Down's syndrome baby to be one of the worst tragedies of life. In fact, since prenatal testing now can detect Down's syndrome in the womb, many of these pregnancies are terminated through abortion.

In Karen and Monte's case, they didn't know until after his birth that their son Jason was a Down's baby. But they would not have agreed to an abortion, nor did they ask God "Why?" about anything that happened to them. As they discussed the implications of their son's birth, Karen simply came to the conclusion, "God and Monte and I are in this together."

There was a period of grieving over what might have been had they had a normal baby. But then they received God's peace.

"I wouldn't trade Jason for a normal boy, because he's who God made him to be and nobody else," she wrote. "It goes back to the old saying, 'God doesn't make junk.' He's perfect in God's eyes. Do we value people only by what they're worth in the world's eyes? Jason is created in God's image, just as all the people in the world are created in his image."

"What is the joy in having a special-needs child?" some may ask.

"When you have a Down's child you're told to expect that child to perform at the very lowest end of the scale," Karen said. "So everything above that is a giant step—a great accomplishment. Every little thing Jason does is a triumph. You do work hard—in therapy—for those triumphs, but there's great joy in it."

Karen has a promise from Scripture for her son, based on 1 Corinthians 1:5: "For in him [Christ] you have been enriched in every way—in all your speaking and in all your knowledge." She prays that verse over Jason regularly for his speech and knowledge to improve. Now she and her seven-year-old daughter are praying together for Jason's finicky appetite to improve. Their family has already prayed him through an obstructed bowel, colostomy surgery, then reversal of the colostomy a year later.

Unlike many congenital disorders, Down's syndrome is not a terminal condition. The child can live a relatively normal life at home, and in many cases go to school, learn to read, and hold a job.

"What is so refreshing to us—and I believe to the Lord, too—is their innocent, childlike qualities," Karen said. "All they say and do, even as they grow older, is precious to the Lord. We 'normal' people lose that as we grow up. All the answers to prayer we've seen through these first four years of Jason's life have increased our faith."

Dealing With Rebellion

For a mother, seeing her own children turn away from the Christian faith she's sought to cultivate in them brings both pain and guilt. Wherever we go, women ask for prayer and share their concern for a son or daughter who has rebelled against the ways of God.

The experience Shirley shared with me (Ruthanne) about her son's rebellion is a scenario we hear about all too often in Christian families. She and her husband, Roger, had reared their boys in a strong church setting and enrolled them in Christian schools. Kevin, the oldest, was especially bright and creative. He sometimes challenged authority, though not in a contentious way. Basically, he was a well-behaved kid.

Then the family moved from one city to another, and Kevin changed schools at age fourteen. He joined the new church youth group and made new friends there, but a cloud of depression seemed to gradually settle over him. He'd always been a good student, but his grades started slipping as he spent more and more time with a new set of friends from outside the church. He began listening to heavy-metal music, breaking curfew, and becoming hateful, abusive, and belligerent toward his parents.

Shirley felt her son was becoming a different person, and she and Roger were powerless to stop it. She discussed the problem with the youth minister—the only adult Kevin would talk to. He referred her to Joyce, a Christian counselor. Shirley also sought help from the counselor on how she and her husband could handle the crisis.

"Joyce helped me see that in addition to the professional treatment Kevin needed, this was a prayer project," Shirley said. "She gave me a copy of your book *A Woman's Guide to Spiritual Warfare*, and through reading it I saw that we were in a battle with Satan for our son. I went into his room and removed posters and albums from the rock groups he was listening to. He was furious, but my husband and I just told him, 'You know it's wrong—and we won't tolerate this in our home.'

"I began paying close attention to what was going on when Kevin was at home, and one day I overheard him arranging a drug buy on the phone. When I confronted him and demanded that he hang up, he slammed the phone down, threatened to run away, and stormed out of the room in an angry tirade. He lit up a cigarette and started burning himself with it, then went into the bathroom to look for pills he could overdose on. I called my husband to come home from work, then called the counselor, and she told us to take him to the hospital."

From the emergency room, Kevin was admitted to the psychiatric wing for evaluation. Shirley and Roger were totally shocked when the doctors told them Kevin had been doing drugs for some time and was suicidal. His listening to heavy-metal music only encouraged his rebellion against all authority, and after watching self-mutilation movies he had begun hurting himself. He'd told the doctors he hated his parents and wanted to die.

Spending a week in the psychiatric ward, and seeing the

condition of other patients there, was like a wake-up call for Kevin. The doctors put him on medication for depression and he gradually improved over that summer. But he continued to dress and behave like the heavy-metal rock stars he wanted to imitate—including wearing makeup. One guy in the bad group of friends who was obsessed with Kevin kept pursuing him and promising they would form a rock band and produce an album. It was hard for Kevin to resist, but he kept seeing the counselor through the summer.

As the opening of school approached, the great pressure of trying to live in two worlds overwhelmed Kevin. Relapsing into deep depression, he agreed to enter a psychiatric hospital for a month of treatment. While her son was hospitalized, Shirley again thoroughly searched his room and removed and destroyed all the heavy-metal paraphernalia. She prayed over his room, bed, desk, chair, and stereo—using anointing oil as she went.

"After Kevin was out of the hospital and back in school, the Holy Spirit faithfully showed me when I needed to check on something and led me how to pray," Shirley said. "One day I felt prompted to search the bathroom and discovered Kevin had been doing cocaine. Our youth minister had resigned and moved away, which seemed to push Kevin into a downward spiral. Then he got together with his old friends again, and the guy who had been pursuing him gave him an overdose of the drug LSD."

That bad acid trip led to a visit to the hospital and was the turning point in the spiritual battle. Shirley and Roger rushed to the emergency room after a 3:00 A.M. phone call to find Kevin strapped to the bed to restrain him. Doctors said they were lucky their son was alive—if another youngster at the drug party hadn't brought him in when his "friends" did nothing to help, he would have died from an overdose. And miraculously, he had suffered no heart damage.

This close call made Kevin realize he needed to turn to the Lord with his problems—the people he'd thought were his friends would have let him die. He saw the concern of his own parents, contrasted with the attitudes of other parents he knew who were aware their kids were doing drugs, but did nothing to stop it, and seemed not to care.

"Gradually Kevin is changing—his attitude, his appearance, and his friends," Shirley reported. "He still struggles with temptation, but he looks to the Lord instead of to bad friends. He's playing guitar in a Christian band and making good grades again—he knows his education is important. He's thrilled he was chosen to participate in an in-depth discipleship study with the new youth pastor. As horrible as this experience has been, we've seen blessings in it, too. God *has* brought good out of evil."

Two basic truths for parents of prodigal children: First, only God knows when a prodigal's heart is ready to renounce rebellion and yield to his grace. And second, we must draw strength from God to help us keep our hope fixed on him, rather than on our heartbreaking family problems.

The Enemy's Trap

Maria is a loving mother who reared her daughters in the church and did her best to instill godly values in both of them. The older girl accepted the Lord at an early age, but for some reason, Katy, the younger, began experimenting with pills at age eleven. Then through friends she met at school, she escalated to marijuana and on to heavier mood-altering, life-controlling drugs. The next several years were filled with fear and anxiety for the whole family as they went from counselor to counselor seeking a solution.

At age seventeen, Katy entered a secular resident rehabilitation program, after which she stayed off drugs for six years. During this time she got her General Education Diploma, then went on to complete a college degree in England. But toward the end of her stay overseas, she began having dreams about a drug-using boyfriend from her teenage years. Not long after returning to the States, she ran into this old friend.

"Both of them were pawns in the trap of the enemy," Maria wrote. "Katy's drug use began again and quickly increased. Soon everything she had worked so hard to gain was gone: car, furniture, clothes, money, and self-respect. She also lost the trust of her family and friends because, in order to support her habit, she'd stolen so many things from us."

As Katy's downward spiral accelerated, her weight dropped to eighty-nine pounds, and she went to jail several times for drug possession. Meanwhile, Maria was attending Bible studies and making real progress in her understanding of the Scriptures and the power of prayer.

She was struck by the account of the widow who gave lodging to the prophet Elijah, then suffered the death of her son. The widow brought the child to Elijah, who took him out of her arms, carried him upstairs and prayed for him, and God restored the boy's life. Maria especially clung to the words in 1 Kings 17:23: "And Elijah took the child and brought him down ... and gave him to his mother." (NKJV).

For two years Maria prayed intensely for her daughter, wanting to experience the end of the story—having her child returned to her alive. During that time it seemed God kept asking her to hand Katy over to him completely so that he could give her back. But Maria struggled with this.

"I'd pray for him to help her but not to hurt her," she reported. "Finally, I was able to say in desperation, 'Anything you have to do, Lord—anything. Only bring her to you.' I would spend my weekends in prayer, prostrate before the Lord on Katy's behalf. Then during the week I depended on the moment-by-moment grace and love of Jesus to work at my job and function in the day-to-day world. It was during this time that my relationship with the Lord deepened significantly. His Word literally kept me alive!"

The culmination of Maria's travailing prayer began one evening when she had not heard from Katy for several weeks. She called some young men in a Christian ministry in New York who had been particularly helpful during this long trial, and shared her concern. They promised to pray through the night for Maria and for Katy. That very night, surely due to their prayers, Katy was picked up by the police.

Maria had already been through tough times of having to refuse Katy's calls for help because she knew her daughter was evading police. On one occasion she had even reported Katy for theft and alerted authorities as to her whereabouts. But now began what Maria called her "greatest nightmare." She attended Katy's bail hearing and saw her child brought before the judge handcuffed and shackled, then visited her in jail.

"Inside, I was screaming, 'I cannot go through this,'" Maria said. "But the Lord walked me through when my legs were weak and my emotions stretched to the limit. While locked up, Katy did accept the Lord and walked with him for a time after she got out of jail, but then she had another relapse. The next time she was convicted and came up for sentencing, she asked the court to sentence her to a Christian drug rehab center, and they agreed. This had to be a result of the volume of prayer on her behalf.

"She has completed two phases of the rehab program, plus a reentry phase, and is now employed and doing well. Katy has told me many times that she knew God was hounding her while she was away from him—watching out for her, keeping her alive, sending people and situations into her life to give her a chance to respond. I've never met a recovered addict or alcoholic yet who does not attest to the fact that they knew someone was praying for them, or they wouldn't be alive."

What about the fear of another relapse? Maria's lifeline from Scripture is this passage: "He [who fears the Lord] will have no fear of bad news; his heart is steadfast, trusting in the Lord. His heart is secure, he will have no fear" (Ps 112:7-8a).

Maria now works in a drug rehab program, helping young women break free from the bondage of drugs and alcohol. Because of her own tough times experience, she is uniquely equipped to minister to the mothers of these young women who call for help.

"I shall never forget that pain," she says. "These women need someone to stand with them, as I so desperately needed, and I'm grateful God can use me in this way."

When Adult Children Come Home

These days, we see growing numbers of mothers laying aside personal desires and plans to help their adult children—often when those same children are reaping the fruit of their own bad judgment or rebellion.

One mother, Peggy, saw her older daughter's marriage fail, despite her prayers. When the daughter got a divorce and moved back home with her young son, the child suffered much trauma in the ordeal. Peggy chose to lay down her own plans and—along with her husband—accept the role of helping to raise their grandson. Then a few years later, their younger daughter divorced after three years in an abusive marriage. She had no children, but she also moved back home. Both girls went through periods of angrily turning against God, which greatly strained their parents' relationship with them.

Peggy shares some guidelines for how she learned to cope with these painful circumstances:

1. I had to be *honest*—to confess my anger, fear, and disappointment—talking it out first with the Lord, then with my husband and a few close friends.

2. I used Scriptures given during times of seeking the Lord to draw strength and comfort, and as weapons in warfare prayer.

3. I finally learned to quit asking "Why?" and to accept the fact that life is not perfect, but God is a redeemer and restorer.

4. I remembered God's promises to me when I didn't see anything changing in the natural realm. I wrote down and held on to prophetic words from the Lord and used them to build my faith.

5. I learned to forgive when I felt trespassed against, and to love even though I was hurt. But this ability to forgive, and to love unconditionally, came only through intense prayer.

"God showed me that he does not exempt us from pain and problems—but he is near the brokenhearted," Peggy said. "Cards and phone calls from people who prayed for us were a great comfort. In my prayer time God's still, small voice gave me words of encouragement or insight. He specifically had told me about two years before these events that a storm was coming. At times in the storm when I didn't hear his voice, I at least had assurance that he knew what we were going through. I learned that trusting God in the darkness produces patience and perseverance."

After several years the older daughter recommitted her life to the Lord. She now is married to a man who is a wise and loving father to her son. The younger daughter's recovery from emotional pain and depression is taking longer, but she too is being restored.

"This experience has taught me I cannot manipulate God through self-pity, crying, or blaming someone else," Peggy concluded. "He *does* honor faith produced through his Word and teaches us to use it."

A Parent's Rights

Another difficult byproduct of divorce that traumatizes many Christian families is the painful wrangling over child-custody issues. Teresa wrote us about her experience of sharing custody with her ex-husband of their five-year-old son Danny. The divorce courts in her state give parents equal time with minor children, so Danny lived with his father for three days each week, then for four days with her.

But it appeared Danny was suffering because of continually moving from one home to another and never really feeling he belonged anywhere. Teresa and her new husband were getting their fair share of time with Danny, but was this arrangement fair to him?

"My biggest nightmare was that I might lose my son," she said, "but after praying about it, I finally mustered the courage to tell my ex-husband of my concerns. Neither of us wanted to give up time with Danny, and I didn't want to go to court, as the judge might rule either way. Every thought of the possibility of losing Danny made me sick inside and the tears would flow. I was desperate to hear from God and have some peace."

As Teresa continued in prayer the Lord showed her that her situation was very much like the Bible story of two women who brought a baby to King Solomon and asked him to settle their dispute over who was the real mother. He proposed cutting the baby in two and giving half to each woman. One woman protested, insisting the child be given to her adversary—which of course revealed to the king that indeed she was the rightful mother (see 1 Kgs 3:16-28).

"It became clear to me that a mother who loves and desires the best for her child must choose life for him—even if it means not being able to raise him. I realized our son was being ripped in two. It was very difficult, but I knew I had to put aside my personal desires and do what was best for Danny.

"After much prayer and tearful soul-searching, I told the Lord if I had to release my son to live with his father, I would. When I phoned my ex-husband again to try to reach an agreement we had quite a discussion, but in the end he consented to allow Danny to live with me. What a miracle! Only God could have turned this man's heart and caused him to become willing to give up his rights in this way. Through this experience I've learned that God honors integrity, and that nothing is too difficult for him."

Role Reversal

Reversing roles with our own parents is a life transition most of us rarely think about until we're facing it. Not only do we regard parents as being self-sufficient, we've often looked to them for help through the years. For me (Ruthanne) and my husband, John, it was his parents who first needed our help.

After Mom and Dad Garlock moved to Texas following the death of their daughter in California, they were relatively self-sufficient for almost four years. Then Dad's health deteriorated and it became hard for Mom to care for him, so we bought a larger house and moved them into our home. This required difficult adjustments not only for them, but also for John and me and our teenage son, who was wrestling with his own problems at the time. It also created an enormous financial strain.

As managing the household fell on my shoulders, I was preparing meals up to four or five times a day, besides struggling with laundry, cleaning, chauffeuring, and shopping. Trying to coordinate schedules for meals, then cooking to please everyone's tastes, revealed just how much I needed to develop the fruit of patience.

At the time I was heading up an editing team to abridge a seventeenth-century Puritan classic on spiritual warfare, putting it into contemporary English. Indeed, it seemed I had to fight for every minute I was able to work on the project.

In the midst of those tough times when I cried out to God to change my circumstances, he spoke to me through Isaiah

45:3: "I will give you the treasures of darkness, riches stored in secret places, so that you may know that I am the Lord." I learned that for those treasures to become mine, I had to change my attitude and submit to his discipline, just as Scripture tells us Jesus did: "Although he was a son, he learned obedience from what he suffered and, once made perfect, he became the source of eternal salvation for all who obey him" (Heb 5:8-9).

I'd always had a good relationship with my parents-in-law, but living with three generations under one roof wasn't easy. Finally, as Alzheimer's disease debilitated Dad, we placed him in a nursing home, and Mom wanted to move back to the retirement complex. We sold the big house and moved to a smaller one, and our son went away to college.

After Dad's death about six months later, Mom felt she no longer had a reason to live, and her health began to fail. Reading her large-print Bible was her greatest joy, but when failing vision gradually made that impossible, she sometimes became angry that she was still alive. And we had to take more and more responsibility in caring for her.

When Mom had a bout with bursitis in her hip that put her in a wheelchair, we brought her to our home to better care for her. But she would become disoriented and get her days and nights mixed up, so I couldn't leave her at home alone even long enough to go grocery shopping.

As Mom turned ninety-two and got steadily worse, we finally made the painful decision to move her to a nursing home. Fiercely independent, she just couldn't acknowledge that she needed the level of care the nursing home provided, nor adjust to the arrangement. Her agreement was reluctant and sometimes bitter.

Shortly after the move, Mom fell and broke her hip and was hospitalized for hip-replacement surgery. She had no memory of the accident, refused to believe she had fallen, and was convinced the nursing home staff had sent her to the hospital to punish her—and we were responsible for the whole problem. This incident was only the beginning of our painful ordeal to oversee Mom's care at the nursing home, without carrying an unbearable load of guilt.

Over the next seven years she had three more major surgeries and numerous trips to the hospital. The whole time, one of us visited her almost every day when we weren't traveling—taking treats to supplement her meals, reading Scripture, and praying with her. She always recognized us, and sometimes was quite responsive, but gradually reached the point where she rarely conversed at all. Many, many times we left the place in tears, asking God please to grant Mom her heart's desire to leave this world and be with him.

We did have opportunities to minister to other residents in the home. John led one of Mom's neighbors to receive the Lord only a few days before she died. When he would read from the Bible and sing to Mom, other residents liked to gather outside the door of her room to listen. Clearly, we couldn't claim to understand God's purpose; we simply had to trust his wisdom and his timing. Often I thought of the verse, "It is appointed for men to die once, but after this the judgment" (Heb 9:27, NJKV). Only God knows that appointment time!

By the time Mom turned ninety-nine, John had resigned his teaching post at a Dallas Bible school and we were building a new home more than two hundred miles away. Again, we didn't understand the timing of this decision but definitely felt we'd followed the Lord's leading.

A few weeks after our move—and only two days after John's last visit with her—Ruth Eveline Garlock died peacefully in her sleep. "She finally got to take the trip of a lifetime!" I told my many friends who had prayed for her. I had received news of her death just after dropping John off at the airport for a missions trip to Asia. The airline intercepted him when he got to San Francisco, and he flew back to Dallas instead of on to Singapore. It was a close call, but God's timing was perfect.

Mom's memorial service was a celebration of her life. At age twenty-three, she had sailed alone to Liberia, West Africa, leaving a schoolteaching career to answer a call she felt strongly was from God. She and Dad were married in Liberia, and together had sixty-five years of ministry as missionaries in Africa and as pastors of several churches in the United States.

Her love of the Scriptures and her keen communication skills made Mom an excellent Bible teacher. During one mission term she helped create an alphabet and begin translation of the New Testament into the Dagomba language for the people in the northern region of Ghana. After discovering this language had no word to convey the idea of crucifixion, Mom analyzed the vocabulary to find a solution. Taking the word for *covenant* and the word for *wood*, she created a word for the cross—*dapuli*. It became the word Christians now use throughout the region.

Her whole life was an example of total commitment to the Lord and a tenacity to trust him through tough times. Her legacy lives on through her descendants and through the thousands of people she influenced, but I am especially grateful to be a part of her legacy. Now I have inherited some of her well-marked Bibles, and several of her notebooks filled with the meticulously handwritten notes for Bible lessons she taught.

In looking back on those years of caring, wondering, and praying, I can say emphatically—*yes!* God truly has given me the treasures of darkness.

Prayer

Thank you, Lord, for hearing us when we cry out to you, and for your promise to be with our family in our heartbreaking situation. We are trusting you to show yourself strong as our Deliverer and to extend your mercy to all of us. Thank you for your grace that has brought us this far, and for the love that binds our family together. We offer you the sacrifice of praise in the midst of our tough times, knowing you will receive all glory in the end. Amen.

FOUR

Adversity in Marriage

Do nothing out of selfish ambition or vain conceit, but in humility consider others better than yourselves. Each of you should look not only to your own interests, but also to the interests of others.

PHILIPPIANS 2:3-4

Usually to get married means to be transplanted. Always it means to hand over power.

... Love means self-giving. Self-giving means sacrifice. Sacrifice means death. Those are some of the things I've said. I got them out of the only thoroughly and eternally reliable Sourcebook. The principles of gain through loss, of joy through sorrow, of getting by giving, of fulfillment by laying down, of life out of death is what that Book teaches, and the people who have believed it enough to live it out in simple, humble, day-by-day practice are people who have found the gain, the joy, the getting, the fulfillment, the life. I really do believe that.

"Lord," I ask, "help me to live it out."[1]

ELISABETH ELLIOT

*M*ost brides look forward to their wedding day through rose-colored glasses while dreaming of a happy future with Mr. Wonderful.

But sooner or later, newlyweds wake up to see flaws in their mates they'd overlooked before. Dreaming gives way to the reality that happiness doesn't automatically happen. Learning to communicate clearly, adjusting to each other's needs, and relinquishing selfish desires are but a few requirements for a healthy relationship.

To survive the winds of adversity, marriage needs a commitment not easily swayed by every storm of life. In preparing to write this book, we circulated a "tough times" survey to more than one hundred women. We wanted to find out which areas of difficulty have created the greatest problems for Christian women.

Number One was *conflict in marriage;* Number Two was *coping with various disappointments with children.* This result simply confirms what our reader and seminar responses over the years had already indicated.

At the time we marry we may not consciously think, *Now I will be happy because the one I love not only loves me, but is committed to me.* Yet the underlying idea usually is there. Of course this only sets us up for disappointment; no human being has the power to guarantee another's happiness.

Each partner brings into the relationship his or her own expectations for marriage. Each one also brings emotional and cultural "baggage" from the past that affects how he or she contributes to the relationship. No matter how well you think you know each other—even if you were sexually intimate or living together before marriage—the dailiness of life reveals things about your mate you've never seen before.

When these differences arise, you may wonder how the two of you ever got together in the first place! Statistics indicate Christian marriages are no less troubled than any others. And it's heartbreaking to see many Christians opting for divorce because working out the problems is so painful.

But with the help of the Holy Spirit, a difficult marriage actually can become a laboratory in which God's love has the power to bring healing. In the process, both partners, if they're willing to cooperate with God, undergo changes, and grow stronger in their walk with the Lord. It's not an easy road, but the journey toward wholeness can begin even when only one partner takes the initiative.

Problems Yield to Prayer

Our friend Sarah found that prayer enabled her to cope with difficulties in her marriage. She and her husband, Wayne, were Christians, but the foundation of their union was very shaky. When they married, Sarah didn't realize he was bound by perfectionism and a need to be in control—due in part to having been raised by alcoholic parents. If he felt out of control in a situation, he would explode in anger. She came from an abusive home, and struggled with insecurity and rejection—fertile ground for the enemy to try to destroy their relationship.

While their children were still quite young, Sarah came into a truly close relationship with the Lord and began receiving healing for her own problems. Then she determined to stand in the gap for her marriage.

"I set a special time to spend in my prayer closet very early each morning before my family got up," she said. "There I would meet with God in praise and worship, intercession and spiritual warfare. Sometimes just living with Wayne was such a spiritual battle I would be physically exhausted when it was time to pray—barely able to drag myself out of bed.

"Each morning I spent almost two hours in prayer. And the strategy worked! By the time I finished, I would be so filled up with God's love, acceptance, and anointing, I could face whatever challenges confronted me that day. When our children became teenagers the enemy's attack against them was fierce. Only prayer and God's intervention preserved them."

Sarah lived for this prayer time each day. As her children grew older she was able to spend more time alone with God and learned to really hear his voice. She also grew in discernment, self-confidence, and boldness.

"Through hearing what the Lord had to say about me—during my prayer time as well as in reading the Word—I became a confident person," she told us. "Whatever my husband wasn't able to give me, the Lord made up for through his love being poured into me. Also, he revealed to me how to love and pray for Wayne more effectively."

God and Sarah literally became a team.

For twelve years she prayed for what she called her "Christmas miracle"—a breakthrough in her relationship with Wayne she felt the Lord had said would come at Christmastime. After twelve years of looking for its fulfillment, Sarah was about to put aside her hopes.

One October day she prayed, "Jesus, I know I've believed you each and every year that Christmas would bring my miracle. I've not seen it come, so this year I'll just put my expectations aside and thank you that my miracle is coming someday in the future."

All of a sudden she felt the Lord whisper in her heart very clearly: *"I thought you wanted me to come for Christmas."*

"Yes, Lord—yes, of course I want you to come for Christmas! I've never doubted that you would someday," Sarah replied joyfully.

A few weeks later in the Christmas Eve service, as their pastor was praying for the congregation, Sarah sensed God's power upon her and Wayne as they stood side by side.

"It was as if I saw and felt in the Spirit an anchor joining us together," she said. "I hugged Wayne close, and knew something awesome was happening spiritually—as if God was making us truly one in him. The next day, while driving in my car, I asked God what it meant. I'd expected a more tangible manifestation of my miracle. When I turned on the radio, the first song I heard was '*This is it—this is your miracle. This is it—what you've been waiting for....*'

"God did bring my miracle, but it took nine more months to become fully evident in Wayne's personality. Gradually he became more loving and tender, showing concern for my needs. He stopped shutting me out when I wanted to talk to him. Recently we were shopping together and the cashier asked, 'Are you newlyweds? You talk and treat each other like newlyweds.'

"We've been married twenty-nine years, and we now have a beautiful, biblical relationship. We pray together each morning, we fast together once a week, and every night we pray the Scriptures over our children. My husband is healed, and growing more passionately in love with the Lord (and with me) each day!"

Finding Strength in God

Sarah knew her own efforts to change Wayne were hopeless. She chose the best route possible to see her marriage healed:

1. Her prayer and spiritual warfare opened the way for the Lord to change her husband's stony heart. God will not overwhelm a man's free will, but prayer is the greatest force to bring a person to a place of wanting to change.
2. She found her strength in God, and allowed the Holy Spirit to change in her the attitudes and behaviors that needed changing to bring healing to her own heart.

Author and counselor Paula Sandford confirms this truth in her book *Healing Women's Emotions:*

You cannot save or change your husband. That is not your job. Only Jesus himself is big enough to transform lives. The goodness of your love may threaten him, because it makes him feel vulnerable, and vulnerability can be a fearful thing.

... There is no guarantee that a woman's husband will ever change, even if her behavior reflects the righteousness of God and though she may have all the faith in the world. God moves powerfully upon the hearts of His children but never forces anyone to receive anything. Therefore, a woman needs to develop her own strength and power in a growing relationship with the Lord so as to know who she is and how to stand.

If her strength is first of all in God, she can then be appropriately dependent on her husband and at the same time properly independent.[2]

Surviving an Affair

Can God can put a marriage back together in spite of an affair? Even when others say it's impossible? In Elaine's case, she had to make some difficult choices before seeing her marriage saved.

She admits that as an immature eighteen-year-old she married for frivolous reasons: Bill's charming good looks, his affluent family, and his ability to give her material things. But after several years of happiness and three children, he started drinking and playing more golf than ever before. To fill her empty days, Elaine joined a bridge club. Then, for no apparent reason, their business began to fail.

"One by one the kingdoms we'd built began to crumble," she said. "Soon, all we had left was each other, and to our dismay, we realized that wasn't enough. When I begged him to quit running around and spend more time at home, he would turn his back and walk away. Then he came home one evening with a minister in tow and dropped a bombshell.

"I don't think any wife is ever prepared to hear that her husband is having an affair. Bill brought the pastor with him because he said he wanted an impartial witness to what he had to tell me. But my yells and tears and protests seemed not to move him."

At this point the minister began pressing Elaine to say she would forgive Bill. "He's not happy with himself," he said. "I know how you must feel, but ..."

Elaine wanted to scream at him. How could he possibly know how she felt? He droned on about forgiveness, trust, and love while she seethed with anger. Finally she muttered, "I forgive you." But her tone didn't match her words.

How can Bill expect me to forgive him, just like that? she thought. *He's held another woman in his arms. He broke the wedding vow he made to me and betrayed my trust!*

Bill loved his children and his home, and Elaine believed that in his own way he loved her. But counselor after counselor told them, "You should never have gotten married. You are not compatible." Still angry, she took every opportunity to remind Bill of the misery and suffering he'd inflicted upon her. Yet she just couldn't admit defeat and let the marriage die.

Although they attended church regularly, at home their shouting matches got worse, and she was sinking into depression. "God, I can't go on like this," she'd cry. "Bill and I are tearing each other to pieces—please help me!"

About that time she attended a church seminar on how God could change a person's life. As the teacher talked about sins of the heart, Elaine mused, *I know I'm not bad enough to go to hell—but am I good enough to go to heaven? How will I know for sure?*

Then the teacher began explaining what he called spiritual laws. The first one was, "God loves you and has a wonderful plan for your life."

As she listened to his words, something inside Elaine broke. The idea that God really loved her had never penetrated. She'd been told that if she were bad, God *wouldn't* love her. That made sense. But could God love her, this very minute, just as she was? With all her anger and bitterness toward Bill?

At the end of the session the teacher asked Elaine to read aloud the prayer of salvation at the back of the booklet. As she read, for the first time it sank into her spirit that God did indeed love Elaine. She asked his forgiveness, and felt a huge load was lifted off her. She left the meeting filled with God's love, knowing her life had purpose. When Bill came in from an out-of-town trip a few days later, he sensed the difference.

"Elaine, what's happened? You've changed."

She couldn't explain because she wasn't really sure herself. She pulled out the little booklet she'd received at the seminar. After reviewing it with him, she said, "Bill, if you pray this prayer, asking for God's forgiveness, your life will change just like mine did."

Bill prayed too. Their focus slowly began to shift. They went to see one more counselor. This one talked of forgiveness, but from God's perspective. As he spoke, Elaine realized she still had not truly forgiven Bill for his affair.

"Are you willing for the Lord to make you willing?" the counselor asked.

Elaine nodded. And with that assent launched the healing process in their marriage. The Lord began showing each of them where they needed to change their own attitudes, instead of blaming the other party for every bad situation. She learned to say often, "I'm sorry." They learned to communicate, to love unconditionally, and to respect each other.

No hope for their marriage? Yes, there was. Because they learned that, ultimately, their only hope is in God.[3]

A few years ago Elaine and Bill celebrated their fortieth anniversary and renewed their marriage vows at a special family gathering. "Bill and I truly are a walking miracle," she says.

The dynamics of Elaine and Bill's crisis are repeated in thousands of marriages. The wife wants intimacy beyond their sexual relationship. The man feels threatened by the idea of sharing his inner feelings—even with his wife. Men tend to think that's a "woman thing." He withdraws, making her feel alienated. She often becomes angry and occupies herself with the children and other interests. Both the husband and the wife are now ripe for seeking comfort outside the marriage.

As we've said earlier, there is no guarantee the husband will change. He still has the power of choice. But if the wife approaches the problem with the right attitude, and depends on the Lord for help and guidance, she does have the possibility of saving the marriage.

Losing Self-Esteem

Tina lived with an abusive husband for twenty-five years, struggling to maintain her self-esteem while he continually demeaned her. Her survival strategy kept her in this situation because she wanted to protect her children and because she had no skills for earning a living. But after committing her life to the Lord fifteen years into the marriage, Tina sought his strategy for her dilemma.

"I had no sense of self-worth," she says, "and my understanding of God's love and the power of prayer was very limited. I walked with my eyes down to avoid contact with people, always fearful of doing something to make Marshall explode. I was never unfaithful during all our years of marriage. Yet any time I answered the phone and it was a wrong number, he suspected some man was trying to call me—and my denials fell on deaf ears.

"I struggled with false guilt, wondering what I had done to cause him to scream such foul names at me. Because of my pride I wouldn't tell even my best friend how bad things were at home—I had learned to put up a good front in public. But these circumstances drove me to seek a personal relationship with the Lord and draw on his strength."

A part of the country-club set, Tina and Marshall seemed to the outside world a perfectly happy, successful, church-going couple. Then when Marshall was in his early sixties, he died suddenly from a heart attack.

After the funeral, Tina discovered his hidden stash of

liquor and pornographic materials, evidence of just how grievous his bondage had been. She also learned he'd had an affair with one of her close friends—the very thing he had accused her of doing. Tina realized her efforts to please Marshall and be an exemplary wife could never have "fixed" his problem, because it was a spiritual issue he himself needed to confront.

Tina shares some of the keys that helped her make it through the final ten years of her marriage as the relationship became more and more difficult.

- I turned to the Lord and he gave me Scripture verses to stand on. One was, "Then you will know the truth, and the truth will set you free" (Jn 8:32). When you are falsely accused it's easy to begin believing the lies; you feel dirty, unclean. But I learned to ask myself, "Just what is truth here?" The truth was I had not done what Marshall said I had done. This helped me to reestablish reality and unload false guilt.

- Another lifeline verse was, "The name of the Lord is a strong tower; the righteous run to it and are safe" (Prv 18:10). I'd simply say the name *Jesus* over and over, and picture myself safe inside God's strong tower.

- Fear was a constant enemy not easily shaken. It was five or six years before I could keep from trembling when Marshall exploded at me. On two different occasions people prayed over me for that fear to lift, and finally it did. I memorized certain Scriptures so I could speak God's Word aloud over myself. Now I'm not moved by what man says about me; I serve only one Master—the Lord—and I know he speaks love over me.

- Today, nearly five years after Marshall's death, I continue to work on my self-esteem. I pray that God's Holy Spirit will cover me, and that any attractiveness in me will reflect God's love. Instead of seeing me as I am in the natural realm, I pray people will see me only in God's light.

Abusive Marriage Saved

Carmen also spent twenty years in what she called a "hellish" marriage, which she figures took place only because she was pregnant before the wedding. Steve would humiliate her and show no regard whatever for her feelings.

After ten years of frustration in the marriage, she had an affair with someone she met at church. "Of course I realize now how vulnerable and how badly deceived I was," she said. "Before my lover's best friend exposed me, I decided to confess to Steve. When he asked why I had done it, I told him, 'Because you never tell me that you love me or that I am pretty. My lover did all the time. I was starving for someone to value me, to give me a sense of self-worth.'"

Carmen repented for her sin, made a new commitment to the Lord, and began praying regularly. Once she asked God whether she could leave her marriage but felt his answer was no. God's challenge to her was, "Are you willing to be made willing to love your husband unconditionally? And to treat him with as much love and kindness as you would me, the Lord Jesus?"

Her response was yes, she was willing to be loving and kind, even if she didn't receive love and kindness in return. But she felt the Lord would not require her to be treated like a doormat. So when Steve berated her, she would tell him firmly but kindly, "Don't talk to me like that—your attack is unwarranted."

After she had done this several times, he began to change. Once he came into the kitchen and said, "I'm sorry for what I said. Will you forgive me?"

When Carmen stopped lashing back at her husband's angry words, he saw he couldn't get into a fight and would back down. Then she would embrace him and say, "This behavior really is beneath you—I know you're a loving, caring man." As a result of her new approach, she's not pouting anymore, and he's softening toward her. As she prays for strength and wisdom, the Lord helps her to respond in the appropriate spirit.

"If you're struggling even to desire to respond to your husband this way, ask God to give you a willing heart," Carmen says. "I would remember how valued and loved I felt by God; then I could give his love to my husband. Now I realize I will never receive my sense of value and self-worth from my husband—that comes only from God."

When Carmen set boundaries, she earned Steve's respect. And God enabled her to do it in the right spirit, while at the same time esteeming her husband.

Any woman contending with an abusive marriage, as these

women have, should call her abuser to accountability. When his behavior is out of line you may choose to say, "I will not accept your accusation of _____," and name what it is that you will not accept.

Women need to know that they do not deserve verbal abuse, and they need not tolerate it. If you are being victimized, tell your husband you will not respond to him as you have in the past—no more yelling back or giving him the silent treatment.

Explain that you want a good marriage, but now you're requiring respect from him and establishing limits. And if he oversteps those boundaries, there will be consequences. When his behavior is inappropriate and unacceptable, tell him so firmly but kindly. You may need to take similar steps to protect your children, if your husband is verbally abusing them. Like Helen, whose story we shared in chapter two, you may conclude separation or divorce is the only alternative.

If your husband remains abusive, don't blame yourself—it is not your fault. But it is wise to establish a plan for getting to a place of safety in case the abuse becomes physically threatening.

Pornography Threatens Marriages

We are dismayed by the growing numbers of women who tell us their husbands are involved with pornography. Many say they became aware something was wrong when their husbands began spending huge blocks of time at their home computers exploring the Internet. They simply go online and can connect to all kinds of sexually explicit programs on the pretext of "working on the computer." Growing numbers of men—and sometimes women too—are becoming addicted to "cybersex."

Once hooked, he begins staying away from home more, claiming he has to work late, then going to X-rated theaters or picking up prostitutes. Or he will indulge his habit at home in the middle of the night. His "public face" is quite convincing, but an astute wife knows an evil force is slowly shredding the very fabric of their family. One woman awakened at 3:00 A.M. and discovered she was in bed alone. The Lord impressed her to go into the family room, and she found her husband (a deacon in their church) watching the pornographic cable channel.

This woman says you should suspect a sex addiction if your husband resists being drawn into conversation, shows sullenness at the dinner table, or suddenly suggests or demands perverse ways to make love. Or he may sit staring into space, lost in a fantasyland where his vivid imagination is fed by what he has seen and read. He may give no attention to your interests or needs—only his own. You may dread going to bed at night for fear he will demand sexual gratification in ways you find repulsive. Your fear may motivate you to regularly be tested to be sure you're free of sexually transmitted diseases.

This is a picture of a woman whose home is being victimized by pornography. For the situation to change, you must take action and set some boundaries.

The "If Only ..." Game

In her book *An Affair of the Mind,* Laurie Hall tells of her battle to salvage her marriage from the devastation caused by her husband's twenty-year addiction to pornography. She describes the insidious ways a wife is made to feel the problem really is her fault—by her husband, and sometimes even by well-meaning counselors. The "If only ..." routine heaps false guilt on her head.

If only I could be better in bed.... If only I could find out what pleases him ... or what it is about me he doesn't like.... If only I could lose weight and get in shape.... If only I could do better preparing meals and keeping house.... If only I could make him proud of me....

These mind games can make a woman doubt her own sanity. And even if she could fulfill all those fantasies, it would never free her husband from his addictive bondage. While Laurie never divorced her husband, she did separate from him for a while.

Her own heartache, coupled with her husband's refusal to get help for a problem stemming from his teenage years, made it impossible for her and her children to live a normal life. Only after the separation did he take responsibility for his actions and begin seeking help to get free.

Laurie writes that at one time her husband had been a brilliant engineer in a top management position, with all the perks that went with it. But after indulging for so long in fantasy, he became incapable of thinking clearly or solving even simple problems. He lost his job and ended up working on a production line for a low hourly wage.[4]

One way Laurie coped was to sit down with a cup of tea and pour out her hurt to the Lord aloud. In these talks she released her right to get even, leaving vengeance to the Lord. She had to continually remind herself of her own self-worth, declaring she was accepted and precious in God's eyes.

Then one day, she went out behind the barn and piled up some large stones to make an altar. On it she laid all the things she had lost—her home, her youth, her ability to trust, her reputation, her sexuality, her undeveloped talents, and the holidays made joyless by the selfishness of Jack's lust. The hardest part was putting her children's losses on that altar. She wept a long time as she laid them down, naming each loss aloud.

> "These are all the things that were stolen from me," I told Him. "They all belong to You now. I give up my right to have anyone pay me back.... I know that You are able to pay me back, if that's what You know is best. If You should choose to give any of these things back to me, I will accept Your gift with a grateful heart. If You should choose not to give any of these things back to me, I will accept Your no with a trusting heart. I know that You are all I really need."[5]

While Laurie's marriage is still in the process of being fully resurrected, her book finishes on a triumphant note:

I have had to believe that He could raise my marriage from the dead by faith. There was nothing my eyes could see that would prove it. But, lately, I've heard the rustling of grave clothes, and my eyes have actually seen some movement in the tomb. God is reminding me once more that He gives an ever-living hope. That fragile hope will continue to grow as long as Jack and I continue to tell ourselves the truth about who we are, how we are, and whose we are. I plan to keep doing just that—one day at a time.[6]

Confronting the Issue

Another woman who stuck by her husband until he gained victory over pornography wrote us about her experience: "A few months after our wedding when I found my husband's hidden porn magazines, I considered leaving him. But after asking some friends to pray for me, I rededicated my life to Christ and began changing my own attitudes. My husband saw the difference, and started going with me to church. Then he also began to change. But still there was strife during our intimate times. Twice he admitted he still had a problem with lust, and I threatened to leave. But he cried and said he'd kill himself if I did, so I stayed. He assured me he had 'taken authority' over the problem as a Christian and was now delivered from lust.

"The third time I found out he was still involved in

pornography, I gave him a choice. Either he would agree to get help and become accountable to another godly man, or I was leaving him. He knew I meant it this time. That evening he confessed his problem to our pastor and asked for prayer. After he confessed, repented, and through prayer was delivered from a spirit of lust, our relationship changed for the better."

Based on her own experience, this woman feels a wife should confront her husband the very first time the problem of pornography is exposed. Delay only makes the matter worse. She believes because she put off the confrontation, it took her much longer to receive healing for herself, and to be able to trust her husband again.

We advise you always to seek the Lord for his strategy on how best to broach this volatile subject. If God has allowed you to discover such a problem, he also will give you directions on how to deal with it appropriately. You can be firm but loving in your approach. The goal always should be to see your husband restored and your marriage strengthened.

Where Fantasy Can Lead

A renowned marriage counselor told us that the main attraction of "cybersex" for a woman is having someone seem to take a personal interest in her. Suddenly a man is asking about her favorite hobbies, or asking what color her eyes are. This unseen male wants to hear her heart—something her husband may not have done in years. Women can be caught up in such a fantasy world very quickly, as Amy discovered to her sorrow.

Throughout her adult life, Amy had repeatedly dreamed about being loved by men—not wanting sex from them, but simply wanting to be held and adored. She would flirt with any man who would give her attention.

These tendencies stemmed from her childhood, when she had been molested by a relative. With her sense of self-worth eroded, she was susceptible to seeking fulfillment through sexual relationships.

"I married my high school sweetheart because I was pregnant," she said. "I never realized how hungry I was for attention until I got a computer and became addicted to the Internet."

Finding several Christian "chat rooms" on the Internet, Amy would spend hours "talking" to people who came into the rooms for conversation. One night she was online and met a very nice man who lived hundreds of miles away. Over the course of three months they spent hours talking to each other.

"One day I gave him my phone number and he started calling me," Amy reported. "At first our conversations centered around our faith. But soon they became more personal and intimate. Before I realized what was happening, I was involved in an online affair. We talked about things I never discussed with anyone, not even my husband. I actually thought I was falling in love with this man."

One day the guilt of her actions caught up with Amy, and she admitted her need for help. Her church was having a women's retreat, so she decided to go and try to get her life right with God again.

"When I confessed to some of the ladies what I had been involved in, I expected a rebuke from them," she said. "But what I got was loving concern and care. They did make it clear that my actions were sinful, but they didn't condemn me. They prayed with me and helped me better understand the reasons I had the 'need' to find acceptance in this way.

"It hasn't been an easy road, but I have been reconciled with God, and he has restored me. I have confessed my wrong to my husband and he has forgiven me. Sometimes I still have a hunger for attention, but now I know how the enemy works, and what to do about the attack."

Marriage problems have no easy answers. But it is possible to build God-honoring relationships on a foundation of sacrificial love and a willingness to receive God's help and healing.

Prayer

Father, I bring to you today the broken areas of my marriage and ask you to begin a work of restoration. Forgive me for trying to control my husband, instead of committing him to your loving hands. Reveal my own wrong attitudes that need to be more loving and Christlike. Lord, I ask you to send across my husband's path a wise counselor who will speak the Word of God into his life. Reveal your great love to both of us, and extend to us your mercy. Lord, I pray you will cause our marriage and our home to bring glory and honor to you. I ask in Jesus' name, Amen.

FIVE

Overcoming Betrayal and Divorce

Even my own familiar friend in whom I trusted,
Who ate my bread,
Has lifted up his heel against me.

PSALM 41:9, NKJV

When you decide to live like Christ among the selfish and strong-willed, God will honor your decision, but ... you will encounter misunderstanding and mistreatment. You will be taken advantage of. However, don't make another wrong assumption by thinking that if you are going through tough times, you are off target. Not so. Doing what is right is never a stroll through a rose garden. Jesus' plan for living may be simple, but it is not easy.

... No matter how painful it may be, let us trust Him to bring good from our living His way.[1]

CHUCK SWINDOLL

*I*t's probably safe to say every Christian woman will be rejected or betrayed at some time in her life. You have likely experienced the knife-in-the-back feeling that hits when a person you have really trusted turns against you.

Jesus was betrayed by one of his close followers. Of all the suffering Jesus endured on earth, perhaps the most hurtful was being denied and betrayed by the very people who claimed to be loyal to him. The pain of disappointment he felt—when Peter, James, and John fell asleep instead of praying with him; when Judas greeted him with a kiss of betrayal; when Peter denied he even knew Jesus—must have exceeded the physical pain of the thorns, the whip, or the nails.

Many, many times women have shared with us their stories of betrayal. Often they say, "If an unbeliever had done this to me, it wouldn't be as hard to take. But this person claims to be a Christian! How can he lie like that?" Here's just a sampling of these stories:

- After her husband's death, a woman learns that a younger woman she had befriended had been carrying on an affair with her husband. She feels betrayed by her husband as well as by her close friend.

- Several women in a church (mainly the widows) invest most of their assets in a Christian businessman's "guaranteed" venture to provide for their retirement. But the man turns out to be a fraud, and the women lose their life savings.

- A woman leading her church's prayer ministry is stripped of her leadership position because the pastor fears too many people in the congregation are looking to her for spiritual counsel.

- A woman confides to her pastor that her husband has AIDS. She asks him to keep the information confidential until she can relocate her children to protect them from public derision. At first he agrees, then changes his mind. On that same day, he makes a public announcement to the entire congregation.

- A young woman who has suffered a sports injury is befriended by her youth pastor—also a sports trainer. She accepts his offer to help her with physical therapy so she can get off crutches. Then, after several sessions, he sexually assaults her.

- A woman at home alone greets a trusted Christian friend who drops by. But he doesn't leave until he has chased, caught, and raped her. She struggles to comprehend how a close friend and supposedly staunch Christian could do such a thing.

Betrayal comes in diverse forms, as the above examples reveal. Though your own situation may not be as extreme as some of these, possibly you are struggling to sort out a potpourri of emotions that come on the heels of betrayal—heartache, embarrassment, disappointment, anger, bitterness, shame, remorse, or guilt. One woman who experienced betrayal by a trusted coworker wrote, "God has always worked all things to the good for me—whether those things seemed to me good or bad. He cannot mistreat me because he loves me perfectly. I've learned that my crises and problems are an opportunity to see God intervene, and he is glorified in the process."

One of our prayer partners cared for her father and stepmother through years of declining health and many medical emergencies. After her father died, a relative of the stepmother convinced her to change the will, depriving the daughter of her inheritance. She wrote, "After months of struggling over the betrayal, God finally set me free to totally trust him to be our provider. Then I was able to fully forgive."

Another friend, who had been hurt and betrayed by her pastor, said she was so devastated she cried for three months. But through that test she experienced a small taste of the fellowship of Jesus' suffering. Gradually she came to the point where she could forgive her pastor. "My journey to healing was a process that took time," she said, "but when it was over I no longer had a sore heart, because I had truly forgiven."

A reader told us that speaking Scriptures aloud and listening to quiet worship music comforted her through the pain of betrayal, and helped to keep her focus on the Lord instead of on her circumstances. Another found peace by writing her prayers in letters to God, pouring out her anger, hurt, and confusion, then asking for his forgiveness and healing.

The Betrayal of Divorce

Perhaps you or someone close to you has suffered one of the worst of all betrayals—when a husband announces, "I don't love you anymore. I want a divorce and the freedom to live my own life." A reader who went through such a divorce called it "the most shameful form of betrayal." She didn't tell her family until she had suffered emotional abuse for more than twenty years. When her dad asked why she hadn't told him sooner, she replied, "Because I couldn't face the shame of failure." But finally, they divorced and her husband remarried right away.

"Divorce is worse than death—it is a deep wound of rejection," Lonnie wrote, responding to our survey. "To realize the one you've pledged your love to has betrayed your trust is emotionally shattering—and it's hard to feel you can ever trust anyone again."

When Lonnie married, her husband had convinced her he was a believer. But his attitudes and behavior soon revealed he had deceived her. Over the next eleven years Lonnie prayed he would commit his life to Christ, but eventually he filed for divorce.

"It wasn't easy to release the marriage after praying so long for restoration," she said. "Through prayer and worship I had to give the Lord my hurt and disappointment—a process that continued over many months. But finally, Jesus has healed me and helped me let go of the past to embrace a brighter future. His love uprooted a lifelong tree of rejection in my heart and set me free."

The Trauma of Divorce

For a Christian woman, going through a divorce and the tough times of its aftermath is terribly traumatic—especially when she has tried every possible means of salvaging the marriage. For some, they realize too late that their own shortcomings and character flaws contributed in part to the marriage's failure.

The church has long held the view that divorce is wrong except in cases of adultery. But I (Quin) remember the scene in my living room some years ago when Cherie, a young, newly divorced woman with a brilliant career, sobbed out her story.

"Yes, God hates divorce. The Bible says so—and most of my Christian friends reminded me of it when I got a divorce," she cried. "But few people read the verses before or after that phrase—where God says he hates it when a man breaks faith with his wife, or practices violence."

She shared accounts of horrible verbal and emotional abuse she had suffered during five years of marriage. One day when she could take it no longer, Cherie cooked up a batch of food for the freezer and ironed all her husband's clothes. She wrote him a good-bye note begging him to get counseling, and left.

After the separation, she gave him time to seek help from a counselor, or to take steps toward restoring their relationship. When her husband refused, they divorced, and he soon married again. Though Cherie had prayed for reconciliation, she came to realize God would not override a man's freedom to choose. And her husband chose not to go God's way.

A few years later Cherie remarried. Now she and her second husband have two lovely children, and theirs is one of the most Christlike families I've ever met.

Violence and Treachery

As Cherie pointed out, we need to look at God's statements regarding divorce in its context:

> "I hate divorce," says the Lord God of Israel, "and I hate a man's covering himself with violence as well as with his garment," says the Lord Almighty. So guard yourself in your spirit, and do not break faith (Malachi 2:16).

Sadly, multitudes of women suffer violence at the hands of their husbands—even Christian men. We encounter this problem across our nation as scores of these women come to us for prayer and help.

When I (Quin) discussed this issue with a well-known marriage counselor, he mentioned a Scripture I hadn't considered: "'Thou shall not kill' is one of the Ten Commandments," he said. "But many men are guilty of killing their wife's soul—her mind, will, and emotions, and even her human spirit—with sharp, hateful, accusing barbs. Words are powerful and they can be very harmful."

In his book *Restoring Innocence,* Alfred Ells, founder of a

Christian counseling service, writes, "Many think they must carry the burden of their wounds alone. But self-sufficiency rules out God-dependency. You cannot rely on yourself to fix yourself if what you need is God's healing.... Have courage. Start slow. You only need to take one step at a time ... but you must take the first step of admitting to yourself, another person, and God your need for help and healing."[2]

A Cry for Deliverance

Consider the dilemma in this next woman's story. Her husband had "killed" her in almost every area of her soul.

"I want to be delivered," the small, middle-aged woman said softly, staring at the floor. I (Quin) strained to hear her timid voice. Her self-esteem was so low she couldn't look me in the eye.

"Of what?" I asked.

"Getting no respect at home," she answered. "My husband ties me up to have sex. He says it is the only way he is satisfied. My teenage sons show me no respect either. When I ask them to do something, they scream for me to 'shut up' as they curse and call me filthy names because I am 'only a woman,' they say."

"How long have you allowed your husband to tie you up?"

"For twenty years. But I want to get set free—tonight."

Obviously she would not see an overnight deliverance from a bondage that had been twenty years in the making. It would take time and deep counseling. Hopefully, her husband would be willing to get help, too. Although she had tolerated his abusive behavior for too many years, now there was hope, because she was acknowledging her problem, and she desired to be free. She did have value. She did deserve respect. Since she was created in the image of God, he did have a purpose for her. And she did not deserve to be treated as a "thing."

This woman's case was rather unusual, but she had tolerated abuse for all those years because she thought it was part of her wifely duty. One who has been taught to "submit" to her husband no matter what he demands is hesitant to go to anyone for help when she's being abused. Especially a church leader. Christian author Carolyn Driver writes: "Your husband may be your matrimonial head, but Jesus alone is the spiritual head of those who love and serve him.... If an act violates the Spirit of God within you, you are not required to perform it. Wives are not doormats or docile nobodies; they are co-laborers with their husbands. We are to submit to each other in love, as unto Christ."[3]

Abusive Behavior

Domestic abuse is a crime that has reached tragic proportions in the United States. The director of the Family Service Association of San Antonio, Texas, says: "Battering by male partners is the single most common source of injury to women, more common than auto accidents, mugging and rape by a stranger combined.... Nearly 30 percent of all female homicide victims and 26 percent of rape and sexual assault victims were attacked by an intimate partner."[4]

"An abuser is obsessed with controlling and supervising the details of another person's life, putting the focus on that person's behavior, rather than on his own faults or weaknesses," a Christian abuse counselor told us.

"He often uses emotional manipulation—tears, blame-shifting, anger, threats, or even silence to control his victim. He usually isolates the victim from friends and family, and so intimidates her that she feels powerless to stop the mistreatment or find help from outside the home. The church needs to take a stand against men who perpetrate such abuse against women and children," she continued.

Too often Christian leaders tell victims of family violence, "You must forgive your abuser and be reconciled." Eventually forgiveness must come, yes. But leaders must require the abuser to take responsibility for his behavior, agree to counseling, and become accountable to a counselor or pastor. Not all marriages involving an abuser can be reconciled.

In their book *Women, Abuse and the Bible,* authors Kroeger and Beck say:

When females don't trust themselves, they more easily give up their power and lose their ability to confront and resist destructive things done to them or their children.

... The abuser can use the church for the same end. Congregation members may see him as a very nice and charming man—this is the facade that he presents to the public world. When the wife tells a church leader of the abuse, that person may have difficulty believing her because the abuser is known to be so nice.[5]

Be aware that physical abuse usually begins as verbal abuse. Pat Evans, a communications consultant, says in her book *The Verbally Abusive Relationship:* "Early in the relationship, the verbal abuser may abuse his partner with put-downs disguised as jokes and with withholding; gradually, other forms of verbal abuse are added.... In many, many cases, verbal abuse escalates into physical abuse which may also begin subtly as 'accidental' shoves, pushes, bumps, etc., which then escalate into overt physical battering."[6]

We feel God's best is for marriages to remain intact, and his plan is for children to grow up with both a mother and a father in the home. We'd never deny that. But we all know women who stayed in a marriage for the sake of the children—while enduring inexcusable abuse themselves and causing the children to suffer great emotional damage.

Things can be made better. You need not remain locked in today's circumstances. Our counsel for you—if you are in an abusive situation—is twofold:

1. Ask God for the wisdom you need to take appropriate action (see Jas 1:5). He does hear and answer prayer—though not always in the way we desire.

2. It's important for you to act by reaching out to contact others:
   - to pray and counsel with you,
   - to provide a temporary safe haven,

- to reinforce you in a confrontation, separation, or divorce if the abuser rejects all suggestions for how he can receive help for his problems.

God Restores and Heals

Tough times need not last for always. We can find encouragement through prayer with special friends, through Scripture, through wise counsel from mature leaders. We can find solace in a sermon, a book, a walk in the park, a music tape, a support group. In opening our hearts to God and to others, healing can come to the areas where guilt and condemnation have ruled.

For many women, recovering from the pain of divorce is challenge enough. But eventually they face the question of remarriage. What then? Some struggle with the pressure of other people's opinions as to whether they should or shouldn't marry again. Ultimately, when she is emotionally ready, each woman must make this decision through prayer and seeking God's clear direction.

Catherine Marshall, widowed when her son Peter John was nine, wrestled with the divorce issue some years later when she considered the prospect of marrying Len LeSourd. He had divorced his wife after she had had to be placed in an institution, and now he had the care of their three small children.

Catherine refrained from publicly writing about her dilemma. But in the book *Light in My Darkest Night*, published after her death, Len LeSourd shared about it in an introductory chapter:

Catherine and I discussed the situation in depth, talked with Christian counselors and pastors ... receiving a bewildering variety of opinions. Catherine agonized over this, praying about it for weeks.

Finally she shared with me the word she believed she had received: *The Lord is in the business of restoring broken homes and healing damaged families. He hates divorce, as He hates all sin, for the harm it does in every life it touches. But He does not lock us into our sins; He is the God of redemption and new beginnings.*[7]

Len concludes the book with these remarks in the Afterword:

Catherine was His principal agent in my life and those of my children during our 23 years of marriage. She stepped into a chaotic home situation and welded five diverse personalities into a family. It was not a sense of her own adequacy that impelled her.... It was the certainty that God was adequate.

Throughout her life, in every tough situation—the loss of her husband, the challenge of single parenting, the death of two grandchildren, the clash of strong wills in a household—Catherine turned to her Redeemer.... She clung to the simple *fact* of His existence—in the absence of all feeling or evidence.[8]

God Holds Your Future

A major aspect of divorce that seems scary to many women is the feeling they must now cope with life alone. For others, the prospect of newfound independence is quite appealing. But regardless of the causes or the terms of the divorce, it can be an opportunity for you to identify with Christ's sufferings, and to deepen your relationship with him.

In her book *Keep a Quiet Heart*, Elisabeth Elliot says the meaning of being "crucified with Christ" is to give up our insistence on our own independence. She writes, "Here is the opportunity offered. Be patient. Wait on the Lord for whatever He appoints, wait quietly, wait trustingly. He holds every minute of every hour of every day of every week of every month of every year in His hands. Thank Him in advance for what the future holds, for He is already there...."[9]

Prayer

Father, I have felt so betrayed—nursing wounds from the past and allowing painful memories to taunt me. Many times I've wanted to get even with the one who has hurt me. But Lord, you identify with my pain since you too were betrayed —yet you didn't retaliate. Help me to follow your example. Today I choose to begin the process of forgiving those who have hurt and betrayed me:_____(name them). I relinquish my right to get even, and ask you to judge them and pour out your mercy.

Lord, deliver me from fear. Replace my anger, hurt, shame, and sense of failure with your peace. As I forgive, I release all the hurtful memories and ask you to wipe them away. Please, Lord, help me move on with my life, and make something beautiful out of the ashes of this experience.

Thank you that Jesus paid the price to heal the brokenhearted and bind up our wounds. I receive the healing he provides, in Jesus' name, Amen.

SIX

Never Alone: Facing Widowhood

"Do not be afraid; you will not suffer shame. Do not fear disgrace; you will not be humiliated. You will forget the shame of your youth and remember no more the reproach of your widowhood. For your Maker is your husband—the Lord Almighty is his name—the Holy One of Israel is your Redeemer; he is called the God of all the earth."

ISAIAH 54:4-5

This grief, which seemed absolutely overwhelming now, was the means of drawing me into a closer relationship with God than I had ever known before. For it is when we realize our helplessness without God that He can draw us closer. I was driven to more intense Bible study and prayer and a much greater dependence on God as my protector and provider now that my earthly husband was gone.[1]

RUTH SISSOM

*S*tatistics clearly indicate most wives will outlive their husbands. We women know the odds are high that someday we'll be widows. But not many are spiritually and emotionally prepared for the experience.

Lavelda is a friend whose sixty-year-old husband, Paul, seemed quite healthy, often traveling abroad on extended missions trips. One week, while at home in Texas, he began suffering unusually severe headaches, and within a few days a brain aneurysm took his life. He never knew he had such a serious health problem.

Certainly Lavelda was not emotionally prepared for this trauma. But as she rebuilds her life and her identity, she is drawing on her spiritual reserves and relying on her basic philosophy: *We serve a faithful God.*

"I have to believe that I'll be okay, and God will still keep me in his peace and love, even though my love of forty-two years has just gone home to Jesus," she wrote. "I tend to want to control situations to obtain the results I want, when I want. But over the years, through lots of heartaches, I've learned my circumstances are not a measuring stick for God's love. When I'm going through tough times, or the end results are disappointing, it does not mean God doesn't love me as much as he loves someone else.

"Once I got past wondering if God was mad at me, I could receive comfort from his Word. I had to decide to believe that he meant just what he said, and refuse to be robbed by doubt. Now I realize he loves me as much as I will allow him to in any circumstance."

Lavelda agrees it helps to have friends and a church family

who will pray with you and for you until you know in your heart you've released the situation into God's hands. That's the hard part, of course.

The Release of Tears

In the midst of writing this book, I (Ruthanne) made a ten-day trip to Tulsa, Oklahoma, to help my mother move into a small apartment. Just over a year had passed since my father's death, and my brother and I were concerned about her living alone in a declining neighborhood. Our prayers were answered when she cleared the waiting list for an apartment in a church-operated complex providing special help for the elderly.

Yet it was hard for her to leave the house she and Dad had lived in together for more than half of their sixty-three years of marriage. To see her usually orderly living room in such disarray and piled high with boxes brought tears. Deciding what to do with Dad's old recliner brought tears. Unexpectedly finding a long-forgotten memento or gift brought a flood of memories and tears.

"I'll be all right—I just need to cry a little bit," she would say when I tried to comfort her. Through the release of tears, she seemed to find strength for the next decision or task at hand.

By the time I left she was nicely settled in her new place, with pictures hung and everything tidy. She was already visiting friends who live in the same complex and meeting her new neighbors, all of them also widows. Then she volunteered to play the piano for the Sunday vespers service. She had closed one chapter of her life with tears, and is now opening a new one.

Rather than trying to hold back your tears, Paula Sandford suggests that crying when you need to cry is important to the healing process. She writes:

> I encourage you to let the tears flow when you have something to cry about, and not to believe anyone who tells you that grief and sorrow are a sign of lack of faith or a work of the devil. The ability to cry is a gift of God. Those who receive that gift and allow it to work in them appropriately are much less likely to suffer from high blood pressure, ulcers, nervous breakdowns, or depression than those who suppress and control their emotions to put forward a courageous front.
>
> … Emotional healing does not usually happen instantly. God respects your feelings, your need to grieve for a while.[2]

Time Is Precious

In our book *A Woman's Guide to Spiritual Warfare,* we shared the story of author Jamie Buckingham's battle with cancer. God did answer prayer in extending his life, but in 1992 he went to heaven to meet his Lord.

Our friend Jackie, his widow, recently shared with us her struggle to adjust to living without Jamie. They'd been married for thirty-eight years.

"I wish I had looked ahead, because life is so short—like a vapor," she said. "Had I looked ahead, I would have spent more precious time with Jamie doing the things he enjoyed doing. When you are married, you become one. Then when your mate is gone, it seems as if half of you is gone. I felt like a part of me had been amputated.

"It is God's grace and mercy that have kept me going. I could have pulled the covers over my head and been depressed. But I had to make a choice to believe God has a purpose and plan for me even now. I'd wake up in the middle of the night praying the *Jesus Prayer*—'Jesus Christ, Son of God, have mercy on me!' And many times I've cried out, 'Lord, please put me on someone's heart to pray for me.' When I sense his peace come over me, I know someone, somewhere, has been praying.

"You don't realize Jesus is all you need until he is all you have. I've learned there is a difference between grieving and self-pity—the latter is sin. From time to time I have to ask myself, *Am I grieving over the fact that Jamie is gone? Or am I into self-pity?* I constantly look to the Lord to help me stay focused on him."

Praise Brings Freedom

While sudden widowhood brings shock and trauma, seeing your mate suffer a long illness means prolonged pain and difficult adjustments.

Near the end of 1988, Lenora's husband of thirty-one years received the dreaded news he had cancer. A friend gave her this Scripture, which was to carry her and Tom through many dark days ahead:

Sacrifice thank offerings to God,
    fulfill your vows to the Most High,
and call upon me in the day of trouble;
    I will deliver you, and you will honor me.

PSALM 50:14-15

After Tom's first surgery, the surgeon told them he'd found cancer in the lymph nodes. Lenora was consumed by a spirit of fear when she received this report.

"I couldn't eat, think, or even function for a couple of days," she said. "One day while Tom was still recovering from that surgery, I was driving the fifty-mile distance from our home to the hospital to see him. Suddenly I remembered the Scripture my friend had given me, and I began praising God in the car during the rest of the trip.

"I didn't feel like praising God at all. In fact, about all I could do was cry and say, 'Praise you, Jesus. You are worthy of my praise, no matter what is going on in my life.' I did this in obedience to his Word, not because I felt like it."

Lenora will never forget what happened when she walked into Tom's hospital room that day. The moment she entered the door, the fear left her. "It was a physical thing which I could feel," she said. "When it left, it never returned, even though we had a two-year battle yet ahead."

Lenora's strong faith during this time seemed to sustain Tom. They were able to carry on their lives in an almost normal way, and they didn't waste the time they had left in feeling sorry for themselves, or in fear of the future.

"We spent the time growing closer to each other and to the Lord," she told us. "Not only did the fear leave me that day in the hospital, but I was free from fear even after Tom's death. Never once did I feel afraid when I was alone. I knew the angels were surrounding me, and that I was in good hands. In fact, I'm still in good hands. And I'm still free of fear today."

Many woman have told us of experiences very much like Lenora's—that learning to offer praise to God, even when they didn't feel like it, was a major factor that helped them get through tough times.

Devotional writer Ruth Myers gives this observation regarding praise:

As fire melts unrefined silver, bringing the impurities to the surface, so trials bring the "scum" to the top in your life. When you praise God in the midst of a trial, you cooperate with His plan to remove the scum; when you complain, you resist His plan and stir the impurities right back into your character.

... Through praise you focus your attention on God. You acknowledge Him as your source of overcoming power. You begin to look at your problems from a new perspective.... You have a part in making them the prelude to new victories, the raw materials for God's miracles.[3]

Why, God?

Jessie, a mother who was twenty-three years old, had been married only five years when she suddenly was left a widow. A truck driver had made an abrupt left turn across a busy highway, smashing into the car her pastor husband, Ray, was driving, with Jessie and their two young daughters as passengers. Thankfully Jessie and the girls were not seriously injured.

Totally unprepared to support her girls alone, Jessie moved back home with her parents and younger siblings. *Widow* was a word she greatly disliked, especially when associated with her name. During that first year she stayed mad at God. Why would he let such a catastrophe happen to her? How could he leave her girls without a father?

She grieved so much, she found it hard to pray. Finally, she threw herself across the bed one night and cried out, "God, you've got to help me! I'm not happy with my life."

"The Lord impressed me to read some of Paul's epistles," she said, "and this became my lifetime verse: 'for I have learned in whatever state I am, to be content...' (Phil 4:11b, NKJV).

"God seemed to be telling me, 'You don't have to be happy, but you can be content.' That did it! From that day, I asked the Lord to work contentment in me. And through the years when things would upset me, he gave me the contentment I needed to get through whatever situation I was in."

Jessie had never worked outside the home, so she asked the Lord to help her pass employment tests and qualify for some kind of job. Even though she didn't have the required two years of college, she passed a test for the state of Ohio and was hired. She thanked God for his provision and kept that position for sixteen years—content.

Her mainstay of spiritual strength was to remain active in church, where she played the organ and piano. Years passed. Then during a trip to Missouri to take one of her daughters away to college, Jessie stopped to see her sister, and during the visit met Addison. After a five-month, long-distance courtship, Jessie—now forty—and Addison were married. Her wedding came only two months after her elder daughter's wedding.

During her earlier single years, Jessie had prayed for a husband. Then her prayer changed: "God, I am content. If it is your plan for me to marry, you can bring a man into my life; if not, I won't ask again." And she didn't.

After seventeen years of being a widow, she considers Addison a gift from God. They've had thirty-two happy years together, and both her daughters love him and call him Dad. Jessie no longer asks God "Why?"

Where Are You, Lord?

Mignon's experience was similar to Lavelda's. Her husband, Dub, was a vibrant, healthy seventy-year-old when, one morning, after experiencing only a bad headache, a blood vessel ruptured at the base of his skull. Rushed to a hospital in a nearby city, he was put in the intensive care unit. Mignon prayed he would live and not die.

"I was bombarding heaven with prayer—along with others who came to pray with me," she said. "Then I got quiet while sitting at the foot of my husband's bed, and put my hand on his leg. 'I can feel you, Dub, but you really aren't here.' Then it seemed I heard the Lord whisper, 'He's with me and doesn't want to come back.'"

Mignon lifted her hands and said, "Go. I release you." A sense of peace flooded over her, and she was able to tell the neurologist there was no need to continue trying to keep him alive. The next day she was present when doctors removed the life-support systems.

"I was amazed that I could tend to everything with such a clear mind," she remembers. "Our four children were there to help plan the service and make decisions. As I tried to pick up my life again, I'd look at one of Dub's tools and think, *What am I supposed to do with this?* And the Lord would show me."

Mignon was doing so well handling her emotions, she surprised herself. Then about a month after Dub's death, she walked into the bedroom and saw his picture. *Why didn't you want to come back?* she asked in her thoughts. *How dare you leave me!* Then she had a long crying spell.

"I cried so hard I thought my head would break and my insides might fall out," she said. But toward the end of my sobbing I said, 'Jesus, you promised you would never leave or forsake me. Where are you?'

"'Right here,' I heard him whisper. I prayed, 'You give your beloved sleep—Lord, I am so tired....' Soon I fell into a long, long sleep and woke up refreshed, never to grieve to that extent again."

Then a month later, Mignon found herself in deep depression. For four days she didn't get up and dress, go anywhere, or take any phone calls. "On the fourth day I realized how self-centered I was being," she said. "I needed to go to the grocery store, bank, post office—to talk to people. To get busy. Jesus got outside of himself to help others. I needed to do the same—for my own emotional healing."

One night Mignon dreamed that Dub released her to live without him, and he thanked her for the twenty-seven years of marriage they'd had together. Somehow that dream brought closure to the matter. Occasionally people would ask how long it had been since she'd lost her husband. "I haven't lost him," she'd reply. "I know where he is—in heaven with the Lord."

Today, eleven years later, she is more active in her church than ever before. She has gone to China, Germany, Russia, and Israel on tours and mission trips. Based on her own experience, she has this advice for others:

1. *Be prepared to be alone.* One of any couple will be alone someday unless the Lord returns first. So while you are both alive, prepare a will. Know where all the important papers are and what to do about them—including insurance policies, property titles, and so on. Learn how to pay the taxes and get your car license tag; find a good

mechanic who can help keep your car running smoothly.

2. *Realize that the "first" of everything will be a painful experience for you.* The first Christmas without your beloved, the first anniversary or birthday—anything special to you. A restaurant where you went frequently can be an awful experience the first time you return alone. Once I was waiting in a cafeteria line and felt a sign was hanging around my neck saying, "I'm alone." But when I sat down at a table and glanced around, I realized others were eating alone, too. I began to adjust to the idea.

3. *Get up and try again.* That's what you do if you fall off a bicycle. Do what you used to do with your partner. It won't kill you—it gets easier each time. Instead of waiting for people to invite you to do things, invite *them*.

4. *Have a family member stay with you for a few days.* After the funeral, it helps to have loved ones close to help you make decisions. You don't have to do everything they say. However, it's usually best not to make major decisions for at least a year—such as selling a house, relocating, remarrying.

5. *Have fun.* Be a fun person to be around. I'm not a grandmother who sits rocking babies all the time, though I am available to baby-sit. After a few years I started taking square dance lessons, which I still enjoy one night a week. I'm meeting new people. When someone asks how I'm coping with widowhood, I tell them about Jesus, my companion and reason for living.

6. *Try to live every day as if it might be your last (or your husband's last).* Do and say what you would if you knew it was your last day together. Is that unhappy attitude really necessary?

7. *Realize that being alone is not all bad.* You have more time for Bible reading, prayer and praise, and church ministries. You can now read late at night if you want, sleep late if you want, eat when you desire. Find ways to reach out to other people. You can always find someone in worse shape than you.

8. *Take care of yourself physically.* Get proper exercise and sleep; don't overeat and get sloppy. Eat nutritious, balanced meals. Bathe regularly, keep your clothes clean and neat, comb your hair, put on some makeup. The reflection you see when you look in the mirror has an impact on how you feel about yourself.

9. *Reach out to others.* This last piece of advice is from Ruth Sissom, a widow who suffered the sudden, traumatic loss of her husband. The car he had been working on fell and crushed him, and her teenage son found him dead upon arriving home from school. In her book, *Instantly A Widow*, she tells how she decided to visit a particularly despondent widow in her church, and found it helped in overcoming her own loneliness and grief. "Offering myself in an effort to assist the healing of others had a restorative effect on me. It was the most effective way I found to promote healing for my own lonely heart."[4]

Prayer

Lord, I'm struggling with my anger because this loss seems so unfair. Sometimes I hold on to self-pity—then I'm overwhelmed with guilt about my feelings. Please settle my emotions in the midst of this confusion, Lord, and give me your peace and comfort. You said you would never leave me nor forsake me; I cling to that promise today. Help me to keep my focus on you while walking through this valley, I ask in Jesus' name, Amen.

SEVEN

Grief and Disappointment With God

These [your trials] have come so that your faith—of greater worth than gold, which perishes even though refined by fire—may be proved genuine and may result in praise, glory and honor when Jesus Christ is revealed.

1 PETER 1:7

Human grieving is a personal development, the private drama in which one moves through specific "acts".... There is reason to the sequence, though the griever may feel bewilderment only; and there is motion, though she feels caught in a single emotion. And since this is healing, always and always, there is hope.[1]

WALTER WANGERIN, JR.

*A*lways there is hope! Sometimes it is very hard to hold on to hope when our dreams have been dashed. When we're disappointed with God or with ourselves. When we feel overwhelmed by grief.

But in the midst of dying dreams, we can always choose to acknowledge that *God is faithful.* How can he bring gold out of our fiery trial? At the moment we can't see beyond our cruel circumstances. We may wonder whether survival is possible.

When Hopes Are Dashed

Kathryn shares her struggle in coming to terms with the grief and disappointment of giving up a lifelong dream. When at age thirty-nine she married for the first time, her hopes of finally having children soared. At first it seemed her expectations were in line with God's will, and the future looked bright. But soon she realized her future was filled with uncertainty and frustration.

Her husband, Andrew, a widower with older children, agreed to a vasectomy reversal. But Kathryn was devastated when she learned the procedure had failed. Now, more than three years later, her hope of having children is fading; in its place is a deep pain she feels may never go away.

"We considered adoption," she reported, "but our ages would disqualify us with most agencies. Then a year after we were married, Andrew began to experience depression, which became so severe that he's not been able to work. My dreams of being a mother and serving the Lord in ministry with my husband seem further and further away. The reality is, I am now working to support us, Andrew is collecting disability, and we are very much in a survival mode. Obviously this is not the time even to think about children."

Perhaps you also have had a plan for your life all mapped out, and now realize that plan has to die as you yield to God's hidden strategy. You will find, as Kathryn has, that God's love and faithfulness can keep you steady in spite of your disappointments.

"Deep in my heart I know that God has a wonderful, amazing plan for our lives—far better than my own plan," Kathryn says. I trust God. Because of a very powerful deliverance he took me through during a four-year period before I was married, I've developed a deep, undying trust in the Lord that life's circumstances—no matter what or how difficult they are—cannot shake."

Kathryn clings to Proverbs 3:5: "Trust in the Lord with all your heart and lean not on your own understanding." She's learning to trust him one day at a time, having learned that if she leans to her own understanding, life becomes overwhelming.

"God is doing such a deep work in both of us—why would he suddenly stop and leave us hanging?" she says. "He won't! He says he is faithful to complete the good work he started, but in his way and his timing. Although we've had some very dark days, this experience has deepened our love for one another. Both of us have committed our lives to Christ, and will flow with his plan, even though we have no idea what it is right now.

"God has taken wonderful care of us. An added blessing is that my young nephew has become like a surrogate son to me. His parents are separated, and his mother occasionally lets us keep him on weekends, which we thoroughly enjoy. God truly is faithful, and can be trusted."

Disappointment and Loss

While innumerable women, like Kathryn, grieve over their inability to have children, many others suffer great heartache over the children they do have. Losing a child in death is a deeply painful trauma. But the anguish of seeing your child rebel against the godly values you tried to instill in him or her may be just as painful.

Louise and her husband were devastated when they learned their only son, Barry, had chosen to follow a homosexual lifestyle. Over and over they asked God to search their hearts to help them make sense of their disappointment. *Where could we have failed as parents?* they asked themselves. They had raised him in church and in a Christian home, with loving parents and grandparents.

They remembered that in Barry's teen years, a girl he had really liked had died suddenly of a heart attack. Confused and hurt, he had become angry at God and soon began leaning toward homosexual behavior. Then he decided to "experiment" and fell in with gay friends. By the time he went away to college the die was cast.

"We were grieved by the terrible choice Barry made,"

Louise said. "But at the time, none of us realized it would lead to his early death. He was a tall, athletic runner who enjoyed life—especially world travel and vacations in the mountains of France. After he took a job at a university in a distant state we didn't see him often, but we kept in touch and let him know we loved him. We lamented the fact that Barry would never know the joys of parenthood, nor would we have his children as cherished grandchildren."

The day came when Louise and her husband learned their son had developed AIDS.

"The fear of death was unbearable for Barry, and for us as well," Louise shared. "His doctors thought he should be in a hospice, as he'd been bedfast for four months. But seven of his friends had died in AIDS hospices. 'I wouldn't live through it one day,' he told us. 'Please keep me at my own home.' We agreed, then reorganized his apartment to become a hospital, and rented an apartment across the hall for ourselves. I stayed there, and my husband and daughter commuted as often as they could to be with us."

Around-the-clock nurses assisted them as Barry lost his vision, then developed tuberculosis of the bone and suffered excruciating pain. Special equipment eased the discomfort of his bedsores, but nothing completely killed the pain.

"He must have prayed the sinner's prayer at least twenty times," she said, "but we saw no fruit of salvation. As he kept getting worse, he begged me and the doctors to do something to help him die—which of course we would not do. At one point we wondered whether God had given him up—but we kept praying and trusting God to intervene."

About this time Louise took a break to attend an international women's conference. There she met a friend who shared about her son-in-law, Jack, ministering to AIDS victims in hospices. Amazingly, he lived in Barry's area. Back at her son's side, Louise asked if he would allow Jack to come, and he agreed. After she called her friend, Jack arrived at their door within an hour. The two young men—about the same age—had an instant rapport.

"Jack came almost daily, developing a friendship, helping to feed Barry, even staying all night so I could sleep when a nurse didn't show up," Louise said. "He took our son through the Scriptures over and over—lovingly sharing with him his need to come to full repentance in order to enjoy God's peace. Jack also enlisted many people to pray that he could get through to Barry.

"'Barry, can you see that the Scripture says this?...' he would ask, turning to passages that reveal homosexuality is not God's plan. But Barry kept insisting, 'God made me this way!'

"Jack told him, 'Barry, God doesn't make a human being one way and then say in the Word that that way is sinful. God does not lie or contradict his Word. He wants you to see that the reason you have no peace and are afraid to die is because this lifestyle, this way of thinking, is not according to his holy plan. And when you're out of God's plan, there is no rest, no peace, no comfort.'"

Barry became totally blind and hadn't eaten for nine days. Louise's husband came to join her, and among their praying friends they declared a fast, standing upon Proverbs 11:21:

"The seed of the righteous shall be delivered" (KJV).

At two o'clock one morning a friend called and said, "Louise, I feel you need to go anoint your son's eyes right now and claim James 5:14 for healing." She got her husband out of bed, they threw on their clothes, went across the hall and woke Barry. The night nurse thought they were crazy, but they anointed him with oil and prayed. Five hours later the nurse came flying across the hall to get them.

"When we got to his bedside, Barry was blinking his eyes," Louise reported. "He said, 'I can see the sunlight! I can see the sunlight! Daddy, I can see your face. Mother, you are coming into view. You are beautiful!' When I picked up a bush of lavender heather and held it close to his face, he smiled and feasted his eyes on the plant. Moments later his vision faded and he could no longer see. But that brief restoration of his sight was a sign to us that God had touched him; he was still listening to our prayers."

The next morning Barry told his parents of a dramatic vision he'd had during the night. "I saw this big hand holding a large book," he said. "A loving voice said, 'Barry, this book is your life, and inside it are black pages. We are going to take these black pages out, one by one, and lay them on the table. I want you to confess to me the sin of each black page.'"

Then he added, "Mother, it's amazing! I feel as if I'm already cleansed—is this deliverance? You'd better get Jack here. Now I understand the things you two have been saying to me for three months, and I see that my lifestyle is wrong. I've wasted so many years—can you ever forgive me?"

"It seemed God had supernaturally removed the veil of darkness from his eyes," Louise reported. "God Almighty broke through and revealed his mercy to our son."

Jack came and spent the day with Barry. He later told Louise that Barry very openly took the dark pages out of his book of life and confessed his sins as they spent hours talking.

"In the end, my son truly was born again," she said. "Though blind and almost totally paralyzed, at last he could see with spiritual eyes, and he had peace with God. During the final ten days of his life, he told all his visitors—many from the gay community—about his wonderful transformation.

"'I wish you could see it, Mother,' he told me one day when the Lord gave him a vision of heaven. 'France can't hold a candle to this'—then he described a crystal river like that mentioned in Revelation 21. A few days later he said, 'Mother, can't you feel the wonderful breeze blowing through this room?' Only he could sense the wind of the Holy Spirit. Then he said he saw in his mind a picture of himself running again.

"'Honey, you are standing in front of a veil which is about to part,' I told him. 'When you get off this bed and walk through the veil, you will go running again in your new heavenly body—running and leaping and praising God.'

"'Oh Mother, I love you so much...' he said. I had no idea that was the last thing he would ever say to me. But those final words have been my continual comfort."

After his death, the family hosted a celebration for Barry's life at a local church, and the pastor shared the gospel message of Jesus' love and forgiveness. Many unbelievers there probably heard it for the first time.

"Barry is home with the Lord, and he has no more pain," Louise reflects. "We miss him terribly, but home is where we're all going if we know Jesus. Because Barry surrendered his will to Jesus, God overwhelms us with hope for everlasting life together. His thirty-three years here are a short span compared to eternity. As time passes and I occasionally feel lonely for my only son, the Lord reminds me of the words he once spoke to a friend in New York whose son had been killed: 'I have your son, and you have mine.'"

Knowing His Voice

When praying for an individual's salvation, as Louise and her family did for Barry, we can be sure that our prayer is in line with God's will. But in other cases, God's plan may be obscured by our own desires.

When we're convinced the things we're praying for—our dreams and goals—are truly worthwhile, we easily assume God is willing to help us achieve them. Relinquishing our own ideas to embrace his plan doesn't come easily.

Probably most of us have grappled with doubt and disappointment when we thought we were praying according to God's will, but then our expectations weren't fulfilled. Strong desire—even when it's purely motivated—can hinder our ability to hear God clearly. Sometimes when we make a mistake we can simply acknowledge we were wrong about our "word from God," and no harm is done. But other times, we wrestle to resolve the issue, and the enemy attacks our minds. "What makes you think you heard from God?" he taunts.

Many times over the years I (Ruthanne) have struggled with this question, and gradually have drawn a few conclusions:

1. In most situations, it's best to have confirmation on my "direction from God" from someone who's not as emotionally involved in the matter as I am. His or her objectivity can protect me from deception. And, of course, anything I feel is a word from God must align with Scripture and with God's character.

2. Even when I do hear God's heart in regard to a particular situation, I must acknowledge that God honors a person's free will. Occasionally a person's wrong choice—mine or another's—can sabotage God's best plan. In this instance, I can ask God to do a work of grace despite the circumstances.

3. In some cases, events later confirm that indeed I had heard from God but was mistaken about the timing. Someone once said, "God is never late—but he passes many opportunities to be early." It's important to seek clear direction in regard to timing.

4. Sometimes my only recourse is to release to God what I thought was his revealed plan. My prayer becomes: "Lord, I don't at all understand what is going on. But I release to

you my own desires and expectations in this situation. I declare your Lordship over my life, and I choose to believe that you love me. Please reveal my own attitudes that I need to change, and enable me to do it. Thank you that in the unseen realm, you are working in people and events in a way that ultimately will bring you glory. Lord, my faith is in you, not in my circumstances. Help me to walk in your peace. Amen."

God Sees It All

Recently I (Ruthanne) read an account that illustrates these principles in a practical way. Pastor Herman Riffel had been invited to accompany a neighboring pastor to teach for a large pastors' conference in Haiti. He gave his friend a tentative yes, then asked his wife to pray with him about it. To his dismay, she felt a check in her spirit. Although she didn't think he should go, she did continue praying.

A few days later she said, "Herman, I think you should go after all." Immediately she again felt troubled about the trip but waited until the next morning's prayer time to bring it up. She told him how bad she'd felt about disagreeing with him earlier, but the uneasiness was still there. "I think I was wrong in endorsing the trip," she concluded.

As Pastor Riffel sought the Lord, he recognized the Lord wasn't telling him to go on the trip—it was his sympathy for the Haitian pastors. "God often uses sympathy for those in need," he said, "but sympathy is not necessarily the voice of the Lord...."

He canceled going to Haiti. And when the conference was over, his pastor friend reported to him, "Things did not turn out at all as we had planned, Herman. It's a good thing you didn't go with us."[2]

Because we cannot see the end from the beginning as God does, we tend to interpret circumstances based on very limited understanding. That's why we need the Holy Spirit to guide us. In Pastor Riffel's case, his guidance came through his wife's revelation, and it seemed to run counter to his own perception of the situation. But he was humble enough to change his plans based on her experience. This exemplifies the strength one can find in praying with a godly spouse or prayer partner, especially regarding issues of divine guidance.

The Grief of Miscarriage

Deena and her husband married in their midthirties, bringing with them their long-delayed dreams for a family. They expected to soon be rejoicing in the tottering steps of their first baby. Instead, they found they were the ones taking unsteady steps through the grief of miscarriage.

"Panic came up my throat like a living thing when I first discovered the bleeding," Deena said. "Later, in the hospital examining room, I asked the ultrasound technician, 'Is that the baby I'm seeing?' I knew what it meant when she turned away from the image on the screen and replied carefully, 'We need to have your doctor talk with you now.'

"'Good-bye, little one.' That's what it meant—a wrenching, unthinkable good-bye. It meant that the fuzzy little image on the ultrasound screen would be the first and last picture of my long-awaited baby. It meant that our baby had slipped quietly through a door that swung only one way. We could not follow, nor beg, nor touch, nor even call out, 'Wait, baby, we love you!' This kind of thing happened to other people, not to us. Please God, not to us."

Doctors removed the evidences of life from Deena's womb. Then bouquets of flowers appeared on her front porch. How could this be? On Tuesday she was going to be a mom. By Wednesday she was not. It all seemed like a bad dream.

"I wondered if I would ever stop hurting—if my life could ever be normal again," she said. "My baby was gone; my journey of grief had begun." Along the way in this healing pilgrimage, Deena compiled a list of things that comforted her and brought hope. She shares them to help others struggling with their own grief.

- *My baby is mine forever and is alive in heaven.* Unlike the message proclaimed by our culture, my baby was not a discarded blob of tissue. The Bible is full of assurances that from the moment of conception, we are eternal creations, intimately known and loved by God (see Jer 1:5, Ps 139, Is 49:1). My baby bypassed life here, going directly from my womb to God's tender care in heaven. But that did not invalidate her life. No matter what stage of development she was in, she was a real baby. Today she continues to be a meaningful person with an eternal spirit and destiny.

- *I will see my baby again.* Although it was so difficult to see past the raw pain of my loss, I was not experiencing the agony of hopelessness. Because of Jesus, there was not only hope and healing for me, there was the certain reality of my baby's life beyond the grave. Someday in heaven I will recognize, be reunited with, hold, and spend time with my child. That will be our glorious, long-awaited time for togetherness.

- *My baby's life was not dependent on anything I did or didn't do.* After my miscarriage, condemning inner voices whispered to me that I should have prayed more, worried less, not taken that aspirin, not lifted this or that, not had my hair permed, and on and on. It was the hardest, but most healing thing in the world to finally face the painful truth: the loss of my baby was simply out of my control. Yes, I had been responsible for taking reasonable care of myself, but ultimately my baby's life had always rested with God.

- *God did not let my baby die to teach me something; neither did the devil take my baby's life.* I struggled with whether my miscarriage was God's way of telling me he didn't trust me to be a good mom. It took me a while to see what a lie that was. Others have worried that a miscarriage is God's punishment for an abortion, sexual permissiveness, or some other sin. While our behavior may bring about sad natural consequences, God never angrily punishes us by stripping us of life. The Bible clearly tells us that Jesus' death on the cross ended all God's anger against us. And I don't believe the devil holds the power of life and death; the Bible says Jesus holds those keys (see Rv 1:18). The power that the devil does have is the power to lie and deceive.

- *Discovering that God understood the depth of my pain made all the difference.* I wouldn't dream of trying to run on a broken leg, but after our loss, I felt obligated to try to pursue life as usual with a fractured heart. It took time for me to accept that comforting me was more important to God than anything I could do or be for him. He accepted and loved me exactly where I was, shattered and confused. He was beside me when I felt him and when I didn't, because he promises he is close to the brokenhearted.

- *Talking my heart out worked wonders.* Being able to talk about our loss was the most therapeutic thing I did. I talked to whoever would listen; we also found a grief recovery support group very helpful. I especially needed to express my love and longing for my baby. Without any of the usual symbols of loss—no lock of hair, no photographs, no obituary, no funeral—it was almost as if my words and feelings were all I had left for honoring and remembering my baby. Bit by bit, I was able to say good-bye.

- *I needed to cry often.* The comfort of release and healing found in tears remains a mystery to me. Losing my baby was one of the most vulnerable times in my life; my grief and confusion were far beyond words. I needed to cry and cry and cry some more. I discovered sorrow expressed was hurt and disappointment released. Weeping, as often and as long as I needed to, helped move me into hope and to a commitment to keep walking through this time of brokenness.

- *Being good to myself each day became a wonderful new life skill.* At the time of my miscarriage, I seldom gave myself permission to think much about my own needs. All the obligatory "shoulds" tended to dominate my day. I needed to allow myself to be excused from things like children's parties, baby showers, family-oriented events, or Mother's Day church services if they were too painful for me. I also discovered how restorative "creature comforts" can be. Things as simple as a hot bath, a thick towel, certain fragrances, music, a new book, photos from trips, fresh flowers, a pretty nightgown, a funny video, special places, or a favorite snack were inexpensive but easy comfort measures that soothed my heart. Grief became my unlikely teacher in helping me make time and room for comfort in my life.

- *Learning a few practical things about grief and loss helped steady my heart.* Grief, like an ugly intruder, invaded my heart, upended my theology, ripped through the most intimate parts of my life. I resisted becoming acquainted with this stranger. I began learning about the grieving process from books and the personal experiences of others. I felt less isolated to realize I was experiencing the same stages of grief common to any loss: shock, denial, anger, hope, bargaining, loss of hope, acceptance, and resolution.

No one else was the mother of my baby, so my loss was

unique. But this twisting, up-and-down trail of sorrow was familiar to others who had been there with their losses, and that gave me hope and comfort. I learned no two people grieve in exactly the same way and that the timetable for grief is different for each person.

As with many women, the anniversary date of my miscarriage was as painful, or more so, than the actual event. But after that one-year milestone, recovery accelerated. I remember realizing one day that I was terribly tired of being sad. I felt a spark of interest in shopping for a colorful spring dress. Morning was coming, and I was getting ready to go on.

- *Naming our baby helped me heal.* About five months after the miscarriage we chose the name Amanda, meaning "worthy to be loved." Now we hadn't simply had a miscarriage or lost a baby, we had lost Amanda, a very real little person. So many things we would never be able to do for or with our baby—but giving the gift of a name was our loving memorial. It was our way of saying, "Your life here was short, but it mattered so much to us. We love you—our gift from God—and you will always be a part of our family."

- *I came to appreciate small victories and God's personal surprises.* Driving home from the grocery store one evening, a wonderful realization suddenly flooded my mind. The first face my baby ever saw was the face of Jesus. Imagine, opening your eyes on the first morning of your life and gazing upon the tender face of your Creator!

In addition to these lessons, Deena continued to share: "One day I suddenly realized I was angry at my own body for not giving sanctuary to the baby I had wanted with all my heart. Instinctively, I laid hands on myself and said in effect, 'Body, I forgive you. You are fearfully and wonderfully made; thank you for serving me well all these years. You are the temple of the Holy Spirit, given to me by God. I bless you.' This was an unexpected but important step in reconciling me to myself.

"Several months later I walked by a maternity store at the mall. Suddenly, something rose within me that was fierce and determined.

"I don't know the theological implications of what I did next, but I walked into the store and stood among the racks of clothes. In my heart I said something like this: 'Devil, you are not going to scare me or stop me from becoming a mom. I don't know how or when, but I am coming back to this store one day. And I am coming back here because I am going to be carrying a new life inside. My God is going to help me.'

"It was an unusual way to express my faith, to face my worst fears, and to align myself with God. But it brought great release. And oh, what a celebration when I did return to that same store, triumphantly pregnant and ready to buy!

"Today our home is blessed with two healthy sons."

Prayer

God, thank you that you make no mistakes, and for the assurance you are with us now—whether we're in joy or in sadness. Lord, you promised to give joy in the morning—then demonstrated it on Resurrection Day. You suffered our sorrows. You understand. And through you, Lord, we have eternal life and hope. Keep us from self-pity, but help us to walk in that hope today—keeping our eyes fixed upon you. I give you praise, Lord. Amen.

—

EIGHT

When You Pray for Healing

For we do not have a high priest who is unable to sympathize with our weaknesses, but we have one who has been tempted in every way, just as we are—yet was without sin. Let us then approach the throne of grace with confidence, so that we may receive mercy and find grace to help us in our time of need.

HEBREWS 4:15-16

ROCK BOTTOM

When you're weak, sick, and alone,
When you're not sure of what's happening in your life,
When all you see in the future is a pathway which disappears
    in the fog,
When you are confused by your own thoughts and feelings.
In such times as these there is *still* hope.
The Lord is strong, alert, and involved.
He will oversee the events of your life with great tenderness.
His presence is in the now and in the forever.
God is the Master Potter, who knows how to custom make
    a dream.
At all times our inner life is known to Him and He cares
    and understands.
So trust in the *Rock*.
That's the bottom line.

JERRY L. SANDIDGE

*D*oes God still heal today?

For hundreds of years Christians have disputed this question. Most people believe God, who has all power, can heal. But will he? And under what conditions?

Healing was a hallmark of Jesus' earthly ministry, and also of the New Testament church. Luke says of Jesus: "The news about him spread all the more, so that crowds of people came to hear him and to be healed of their sicknesses" (Lk 5:15).

And the early church was instructed: "Is any one of you sick? He should call the elders of the church to pray over him and anoint him with oil in the name of the Lord. And the prayer offered in faith will make the sick person well; the Lord will raise him up" (Jas 5:14-15).

Yes, we definitely believe God still heals today. Nowhere does Scripture teach that divine healing ended with the New Testament era.

Throughout the Bible, God's people are encouraged to pray for healing, but no specific formula is given that guarantees healing will always come. We simply acknowledge that it is our business to pray, and God's business to heal—whether through prayer, medical treatment, or natural recuperative powers.

Jesus healed people in different ways and under varying conditions, as did his followers. No one can explain why some who seem to pray with faith are not healed. Nor why others whose faith is shaky experience healing. Nor why some receive only a partial healing. Nor why some die what seems to us an untimely death.

But we *can* establish our faith on the validity of God's Word and his almighty power, even when we cannot understand his ways.

In this chapter we share stories of those who prayed for healing with differing results. But whatever the outcome, God worked mightily in each case.

No Crisis Is Bigger Than God

Sharon Spencer is a Texas pastor's wife whose faith in God for healing was challenged by four successive family traumas. Dick—a businessman as well as a pastor—was energetic and seemingly healthy. They had never had a serious health crisis in their immediate family, but many times they had prayed for others and seen them healed. Then without warning Dick was stricken with a serious heart attack.

"The day that happened, my life on this earth was changed," Sharon says. "I felt fear, anger, hurt, self-pity, frustration, and resentment—all at the same time, it seemed. But those emotions were in my soul. In my spirit, I had the peace that only Jesus gives. Over and over, I had to *choose* to let it abide in me when my emotions wanted to run wild."

Five days of hospital treatment, and intensive prayer by friends who gathered at the hospital, got them through that crisis—especially when dangerous reactions to medication set in. Although she had always been a woman of prayer,

Sharon's prayer life increased greatly after this event. Soon Dick was back in the pulpit—vigorous and much more sensitive to others' needs than he'd ever been before. But exactly three months later he had an even stronger heart attack that blocked five arteries.

"The previous crisis had prepared me for this one," Sharon reported. "I again called on the body of Christ for prayer, and the Holy Spirit revealed to many of them how to battle for Dick's life. I cried out to God in my weakness, and again he became my strength."

They rushed Dick to the hospital, and soon a fresh surgical team was ready to do bypass surgery. Sharon was able to release the matter into God's hands when they wheeled Dick into the operating room.

"God responded to our prayers of agreement," she said. "The surgery was successful; the recovery was covered with grace and mercy. Day by day as we kept our focus on him, God's love cast out the fear."

For both Sharon and Dick, the whole experience served to deepen their faith and their witness. But the trials for this family were not over. About a year later, Sharon awakened in the night and sensed an alert to pray for their thirty-year-old younger son, Greg.

"I felt the Lord told me to place Greg on the altar as Abraham did Isaac, and that he would provide for him," she said. "Aloud in the darkness I prayed, 'Lord, I put my son on the altar, and believe you to provide for his healing.' I was aware that Greg had not been feeling well, and had gone for a CAT scan.

"I was at the church when the call came with the shocking results of the test: Greg had a brain tumor. But again, God had prepared me for this moment; fear and shock did not overcome me. Immediately I felt God's peace. He would provide."

Feeling uneasy after consulting a neurosurgeon in the nearest large city, Greg and Dick flew to Los Angeles to seek another surgeon's opinion. The surgery was scheduled for the following day.

"When we were told the procedure could cause death or blindness, I felt a spirit of death was trying once again to invade our family," Sharon said. "We had to rein in our emotions to the peace of Jesus, and remember that the power of prayer could change the atmosphere and the circumstances. During the twelve-hour surgery Dick, and our daughter-in-law, and I waited together. But we knew the prayers of many were upholding us, and I clung to the word the Lord had spoken about his provision. How thankful I am to know I can hear his voice!"

The surgery was successful and the tumor benign, although Greg did suffer some nerve damage to his face and hearing loss in one ear. The first few days after the surgery brought many problems, but as each emergency arose Sharon and Dick would phone home for specific prayer and the difficulty would be resolved. Even in the midst of their crisis, they took every opportunity to share their faith with others in the hospital, and led eighteen people to the Lord during those ten days.

Today Greg and his young family rejoice in God's faithfulness to them. Very little evidence of the nerve damage to his face remains, and they are believing God to restore his hearing.

New Prayer Assignment

When these crises were past, Sharon's heightened interest in prayer continued. Then one day she felt the Lord said to her, "I am putting you on a prayer assignment for your son, Eric." This is her adopted son who is less than one year older than Greg. For some months he had been struggling with unusual stress, emotional edginess, and visual problems.

"To me, this meant more prayer than usual—seeking direction from God's Word for Eric, and doing spiritual warfare for his physical well-being," Sharon said. "Again, God prepared me for what was ahead."

About three weeks after this prayer assignment began, Eric went to an opthalmologist for an eye exam. He called his mother to come pick him up when the exam was finished.

"He got into the car, emotionally shaken," Sharon related.

"'They say I have a brain tumor! Can you believe that?' he said. None of us had even suspected a brain tumor, but I felt as if God dropped a rod of strength into my spirit. His peace completely overcame all my emotions—that is the power of God! I was able to calmly comfort him, then drive to Eric's home to tell his wife and call Dick."

That evening hospital tests confirmed the diagnosis, and once again they sent out a call for prayer. The situation was critical; because of the location and size of the tumor, Eric could have lost his eyesight or his life at any moment.

"But God's timing and direction were incredible," Sharon reported. "Again we were in a storm, but our anchor of faith held. My son had suffered much of his life with a sense of rejection, never fully knowing God's love nor his father's acceptance. For years I had targeted this problem in prayer. The night before the surgery in a Dallas hospital, Greg came to comfort his brother and pray that God would reveal himself to Eric in a very special way."

Countless people at home were praying, and the Christian surgeon—a recognized authority in this very risky procedure—prayed with the family before the surgery. The operation was successful and the prognosis excellent. But Sharon knows God did much more than spare Eric's life and his vision.

"I went into ICU to see him after the surgery," she said. "Eric looked up and said, 'Mom I saw that light again—like on Neely Street.' When he was seven years old we had lived on that street, and Eric had had a dream that he was in a very dark cave. He'd heard a voice calling his name to come out; as he did, he saw a bright light. Then he saw Jesus reaching toward him. His remark was, 'Mom, his robe was whiter than in our Bible storybook.' That morning I had prayed with him to receive Jesus as his savior.

"Now, more than twenty-five years later, the Lord had again revealed himself to Eric. And through our expressions of love and care in his crisis, he truly experienced the depth of God's love and his family's acceptance."

Sharon knew then, and now is even more convinced, that God's hand is on her son for a specific purpose. Eric's recovery has been remarkable; all the things that could have gone wrong did not. And during their stay in Dallas, Sharon and Dick led ten people to accept the Lord—including one young woman who also had had brain surgery.

"I have shed no tears through this tough time, because I've seen God answering the prayers I had prayed in the good times," she said. "Through this crisis, he has healed Eric's spirit, soul, and body. Though his left eye still has some fluid pressure, we're trusting God to take care of that. I'm called to believe, not to worry. My focus must be on Jesus at all times—listening for his directions, obeying his instructions, and not allowing my emotions to hinder or block my faith. God is faithful!"

"That I May Know Him ..."

Five years after a boating accident that caused her to undergo twenty-two major surgeries to put her face back together, Hilda faced surgery and possible death once again, this time due to malignant melanoma.

The cancer surgeon told her he'd have to remove most of the upper arm muscle and all the glands under her left arm. Then he would take skin from her leg to graft onto the affected area. Upon awakening from surgery she heard the grim prognosis: *possibly only three months to live.*

"I returned home in such excruciating pain, I had to move

out of the bedroom because my husband couldn't rest with my moaning," she said. "The skin graft did not heal and boils developed all around it. After God saw me through all the surgeries following the boating accident, I had been teaching faith and healing in churches all around our hometown in Alabama. But now I was facing the loneliest time of my life.

"One day in prayer I said, 'Father, until now I have not asked why the boat propeller sliced my face. But now I'm going to ask you. Why?'"

Immediately Hilda sensed the room was filled with God's presence. She felt as if Jesus sat on her bed and said, "Until now you have learned what I can do for you. Now I want you to know me." She lay there weeping, then suddenly thought of this verse: "Though he slay me, yet will I trust in him" (Jb 13:15a, KJV).

"I repeated those words, and the minute I got them out of my mouth, the pain left," she said. "From then on I began to heal. I was on a new path of not only trusting God, but of seeking him with all my heart.

"Instead of the three months doctors had predicted, I've had twenty-one years of life since that initial cancer scare."

Hope for the Hopeless

How do you handle tough times when a doctor virtually pronounces your death sentence?

Mickie Winborn tells her story: "On a cold January day,

after five hours of surgery and two blood transfusions, I woke up to hear the doctor tell me and my husband, Ken, the results.

"'You have cancer, and I have done all that I can do,' he said bluntly. 'There were tumors in both ovaries, and the malignancy has metastasized.... You've had cancer for at least two years, probably more. The cancer is in its last stages. There is one more thing that we can do—if you will agree to it—called the "gold treatment." It is a live radioisotope inserted inside you to kill the cancer cells.'

"I agreed to take the treatment when I was stronger. Then one evening I felt the Lord spoke to my heart saying it was not his will for me to die, but to live—to bring honor and glory to him. Later a man who came with a friend to pray for me said, 'I believe the Lord will raise you up to help people and be a witness to them, even to travel to many countries.' That seemed impossible—just to live would be a great gift. But I was willing to do whatever the Lord asked of me.

"Two months later, after a preliminary operation, the doctor gave the go-ahead for me to take the 'gold treatment.' To keep this radioactive fluid flowing through my body, I had to be turned every fifteen minutes, and they kept drawing my blood for testing. The results were not encouraging.

"After returning home from the hospital I was too weak even to talk on the phone, and was quietly going downhill. Then suddenly, I had a new problem. Both breasts were filled with tumors. My cancer had spread. During this tense time, I faced the prospect of dying—perhaps within a year. The breast biopsy was postponed until I could regain my strength from the previous three operations.

"With a reprieve of time, I decided to fly to Pittsburgh, Pennsylvania to attend one of Kathryn Kuhlman's miracle services. I had been reading about miraculous healings taking place as she called on Jesus' healing power during her large meetings.

"A friend arranged to accompany me, and we called Miss Kuhlman's office so they'd be expecting me. When we arrived at the meeting hall we found two seats on the front row, and saw that all manner of sick folk were there. Miss Kuhlman preached on God's love. Soon she began to call out various healings as God revealed them to her.

"About midway through the meeting, she announced: 'There is a woman here from Texas who is dying of cancer. I want everyone to forget your own problems and pray for her.' Then she motioned for me to come forward. I felt unworthy to ask all those people to pray for me, but I went forward.

"Miss Kuhlman told me not to pray, but to listen and agree with her prayer. Then she prayed. I didn't experience any evidence of a physical change as I returned to my seat. The tumors were still in my breasts. But the spirit of fear I'd felt was replaced by pure joy as I left the meeting. To this day, I don't know exactly what happened—I just felt changed on the inside. We immediately returned home as I was now facing the fourth surgery.

"During my prayer time the day before the biopsy surgery, the Lord showed me there is a fine line between *divine heal-*

ing and *mind healing*. The source of divine healing is Jesus Christ. I was familiar with the Scripture: 'He himself bore our sins in his body on the tree, so that we might die to sins and live for righteousness; by his wounds you have been healed' (1 Pt 2:24).

"Unconsciously, I had moved into *mind healing*—meaning I was trying to bring it about through exercising "mind over matter." The changeover from faith in the finished work of Christ to faith in my own ability to believe had been so subtle I was unaware when it happened. The Spirit of Truth, the Holy Spirit, had to reveal this to me. Immediately I asked God to forgive me.

"Also, though not consciously aware of it, I had been counting on my good works to merit special attention from God. I repented of this sin of presumption. Very slowly, my heart began to fill with the assurance that I was healed through the power of Jesus Christ and his finished work on the cross. The biopsy was performed. Imagine my relief when there was no sign of malignancy—absolutely none!

"Fifteen months later I submitted to exploratory surgery by the doctor who had performed the gold treatment. Still no evidence of cancer. Years of regular checkups still show no sign of trouble in my body. One doctor said, 'That woman certainly experienced a miracle! She had massive malignancy internally. It was nothing but a miracle.' For the past twenty years I have traveled into many nations and prayed for hundreds of people. I pray the same promises of God's mercy and compassion for others that he gave to me, and I have witnessed multitudes of healings."[1]

Some Are Not Healed

But what about those who are not healed? Many others also attended Miss Kuhlman's meetings and prayed to God for healing, but returned home without the miracle they sought. Joni Eareckson Tada, who was paralyzed at age seventeen after breaking her neck in a diving accident in 1967, went to numerous healing services, but she never walked away from her wheelchair.

Her penetrating book, *When God Weeps*, examines the meaning of suffering, and the lessons she's learned from her own experience. She likens the process to the work of a sculptor who chips away stone to reveal a hidden image. She writes:

Yielding to the chisel is "learning obedience from what we suffer." Our circumstances don't change; *we* change. The "who" of who we are is transformed, like a form unfolding, into his likeness with ever-increasing glory.

...I cannot afford to focus on the hammer and chisel. I cannot look around me and bemoan what God is chipping away.

...Believing in the Sculptor is living hope. Turn your focus on him, trusting that he will never cut or gouge too deeply.... God is not a casual or capricious Sculptor.... He promises to be precise with the chisel.[2]

God's Understanding Is Superior

I (Quin) have a close friend who, like Joni, has spent decades in a wheelchair. Mike was stricken with polio and left paralyzed while serving as a doctor in the U.S. Army.

When Fran married Mike, he'd already been in a wheelchair for five years. They met during his residency training for rehabilitation medicine. She knew when she said "I do" that she would be living with a paraplegic for all her married life. But she never knew God would be gracious enough to give them more than forty years together. In fact, at the time of the wedding neither of them was serving God.

Today, Mike is still in a wheelchair, though many people have prayed for him to walk. Fran says her husband is an overcomer. He sometimes teases and says that's why he's balding—from so many hands laid on his head when people prayed for him.

Do they believe in divine healing? Absolutely. In 1962, soon after Mike committed his life to Christ, a severe pain at the base of his skull baffled the doctors and made him delirious. Fran and a friend knelt at his bedside and prayed for God to heal him. At that same instant, a prayer group in another state also was praying for him.

In moments he told Fran, "I have no more pain! I felt a hand on the back of my head—as though it was pushing away the pain." Later they saw their son Mark healed from Hodgkins disease. For them, healing is very real.

Recently when I asked Mike what he'd learned from his

experience, this was his response: "Though God healed something in me when I was delirious with pain from pressure at the base of my skull, he did not heal all of me. God's understanding of my innermost being is superior to mine. Had I been totally healed I might not have been as useful to him."

Mike has nurtured countless growing Christians through his excellent Bible studies, and Fran is a strong intercessor. Together, the two conduct marriage seminars, helping troubled couples strengthen their relationships. Mike's influence has touched many other lives, including my own during the years he was our Bible study leader.

Wrestling With the Question "Why?"

At the beginning of this book we reaffirmed our conviction that we need to stand against the enemy and engage in spiritual warfare with the weapons God provides. For many believers, the matter of physical healing is one of our most difficult battles. What if you feel you've prayed in faith, but healing doesn't come? Does it mean your faith is deficient? Or that some hidden sin is the hindrance?

When our book *A Woman's Guide to Spiritual Warfare* was released in 1991, I (Ruthanne) wrote about the battle my family waged for my younger brother, Jerry, who had cancer.[3] I am convinced that prevailing prayer and spiritual warfare on the part of many people made the difference in extending Jerry's life beyond what the doctors thought possible. But his death in 1992 at age fifty-two was one of the most painful trials I've ever experienced.

Twelve years transpired from the time of his first diagnosis to the end of his life. During most of that time he was free of cancer, and they were some of the most effective years of his forty years of ministry. He had preached his first sermon at age twelve, then went on to earn five academic degrees, establish an outreach to university students in Europe, teach in two seminaries, and serve as a senior pastor until a few months before his death.

When I got word of the cancer's recurrence, I wrestled with the question "Why?" At the outset of the battle, when Jerry and his family were living in Europe, the Lord had given us a Scripture to stand on: "This sickness is not unto death, but for the glory of God, that the Son of God might be glorified thereby" (Jn 11:4, KJV). Nine months later, and for almost eight years following, Jerry was free of cancer (during which time he wrote the verse "Rock Bottom," which appears at the beginning of this chapter).

With each recurrence—one in 1989, another in 1991—I was again declaring victory based on John 11:4, as our family and his entire congregation prayed for his healing. But the Holy Spirit seemed to be saying that was not the Scripture verse to claim at this juncture, for this time, healing did not come. I sought the Lord for a word of comfort—for myself as well as for Jerry.

I felt impressed to read the story of Hezekiah, and a fragment of a verse almost leapt off the page: "Thus says the Lord, 'Do not be afraid of the words which you have heard'"

(2 Kgs 19:6, NKJV). As I prayed over that verse, I didn't feel it meant Jerry would be healed in spite of the doctors' prognosis, but that he need not fear the tormenting words the enemy was speaking to him.

"Lord, is that the word you want me to share with Jerry?" I asked. The answer was yes.

I wept at the painful reality, but felt a sense of peace that God was in control. A short time later I visited my brother and realized he was tormented with fear.

"Jerry, if you've reached the point where you're ready to ask God to take you home, I'll agree with you," I told him. "But you don't have to go in fear. The devil doesn't hold your life in his hands—God does. And he is not the author of fear." After a period of prayer the atmosphere changed, and he was at peace.

A few weeks later my sister-in-law reported that at the time of Jerry's passing a glorious sense of God's presence filled the room as the song "I Surrender All" was playing on the tape deck. She literally felt his spirit leave his body, moving past her and out through the ceiling. At that moment the music changed to, "I Am Thine, O Lord."

The last sermon he had preached was entitled "Lessons Learned Through Suffering," in which he said: "Difficulties in life should make my faith purer, my trust more steadfast, my hope brighter, and my resolve deeper.... No matter what enters my life, it must never cause me to move away from God; rather, closer to him."

As I write this five years after his homegoing, I realize those words express the fundamental issue at stake: how will we respond when healing does not come, and we go through the valley of death? Jerry's ministry was effective in many areas, but no doubt his greatest impact on others' lives was sharing the lessons he learned through suffering.

Scripture tells us, "For David, after he had served his own generation by the will of God, fell asleep, was buried with his fathers..." (Acts 13:36, NKJV).

Physical healing may not always come in response to our prayers. But we need to make certain that, no matter what the outcome, we will have done God's will in serving our generation.

Prayer

Father, my loved one _____(name) is ill. I come boldly to your throne of grace with confidence, asking that he/she receive mercy and grace in time of need (see Heb 4:16). Lord, I ask you to heal and restore his/her body, causing it to function as you created it to function. Restore his/her soul and spirit, and grant wisdom to those who are caring for him/her. I pray there will be no adverse reaction to medications, and no complications during his/her recovery. May Jesus the Great Physician heal _____(name) just as he healed the sick when he was on earth. I thank you, Lord. Amen.

NINE

When the Cradle Is Empty

In bitterness of soul Hannah wept much and prayed to the Lord. And she made a vow, saying, "O Lord Almighty, if you will only look upon your servant's misery and remember me, and not forget your servant but give her a son, then I will give him to the Lord for all the days of his life."

1 SAMUEL 1:10-11

No matter how we rationalize, God will sometimes seem unfair from the perspective of a person trapped in time. Only at the end of time, after we have attained God's level of viewing, after every evil has been punished or forgiven, every illness healed, and the entire universe restored—only then will fairness reign.

… Not until history has run its course will we understand how "all things work together for good." Faith means believing in advance what will only make sense in reverse.[1]

PHILIP YANCEY

*W*ill *I ever be a mother?* In an era when barrenness was considered to be a curse, these words must have haunted Hannah as she wept and travailed before God. Many childless women of today do the same.

After seven years of marriage, Pam often asked herself this question. Finally she began to believe perhaps God would never grant her this great desire of her heart—to be a mother.

"Spending two unsuccessful years with a fertility specialist made me realize I would either have to undergo surgery for endometriosis, or God would have to heal me," she reported. "I chose to wait on the Lord."

For a fertile woman to understand the emotional and spiritual battleground of barrenness requires great imagination and much empathy. Pam felt the sight of a pregnant woman was an instant rebuke, a reminder of her own emptiness. To her, a baby shower was worse than a medieval torture chamber, with each opened gift mocking her closed womb.

"The enemy uses every opportunity to twist the knife of barrenness in one's back as an accusation of failure," she told us. "If allowed, he will use this imagined failure to drive a wedge between the woman and God—the only one who can help her."

For Pam, a bend in the road of despair finally came. When she learned a dear friend had avoided telling her she was pregnant for fear she was too emotionally fragile to hear the news, she jolted to attention.

"I was ashamed of my selfishness," she said. "Also ashamed that I couldn't rejoice with a friend over her blessing. But most of all, ashamed that I had made God so small in my life that barrenness was an insurmountable obstacle. In that instant, I repented and made an about-face. Within a week I was able to say, by faith, that if I lived and died childless, Jesus would be enough."

A short time later, God unexpectedly gave Pam and her husband, Chuck, a son through private adoption. They had not even considered this possibility until a friend approached them about adopting a child who needed a home. Finally Pam had her long-awaited desire fulfilled: she was a mother.

God had answered the cry of her heart by giving her Daniel. She felt she couldn't possibly love him more even if she had actually given him physical birth. This son was a precious gift and she was content.

But God had not closed this chapter of Pam's life.

"One day during Daniel's morning nap, the Lord spoke to me and set His plan in motion," she reported. "I sat down with my Bible and a cup of coffee for my usual quiet time, and a phrase from 1 Timothy 5:14 seemed to leap from the page: 'I will therefore that the younger women marry, *bear* children...'(KJV).

"God used only a single word to get my attention. But I knew full well if he wanted me to bear children, he would have to heal me. So I embarked on a step-by-step, months-long journey through Scripture, feeling God had promised it would end with my healing."

Through 1 Samuel 1:1-18, the Lord showed Pam the condition of Hannah's soul as a result of her barrenness. Regardless of her husband's devotion to her, Hannah was "in bitterness of soul, and prayed to the Lord and wept in anguish" (v. 10, NKJV). As she prayed at the temple of the Lord, Eli the priest mistook her distress for drunkenness. When he confronted her, Hannah replied, "No, my lord, I am a woman of sorrowful spirit."

Eli's answer to Hannah was the one Pam was looking for in response to her own prayer: "Go in peace, and the God of Israel grant your petition which you have asked of Him" (v. 17, NKJV). As soon as Hannah received Eli's blessing she left the temple and was free from her despair. The word of the Lord had filled her heart with faith.

Armed with this knowledge, Pam went to the office of her pastor in Houston and shared with him that she felt the Lord wanted her to bear children. Without a moment's hesitation, this man of God knelt on the floor beside her and repeated Eli's words. Pam walked out of that office knowing in her heart she had the faith of Hannah. God would complete what he had begun.

About this time Pam and Chuck attended a Bible conference in Dallas and began to experience worship at an entirely different level from anything they had known before. Pam had never felt the presence of God in such a tangible way.

On the third day, as the minister spoke about the believer's role in God's healing process, faith began to well up within Pam stronger than ever before. The minister began calling out various physical afflictions, and asked people to stand for healing prayer if they had those needs. Then he instructed the others to lay hands on and pray for those around them who were standing.

"As Chuck and I prayed for a man near us, I felt intense heat enter the top of my head and radiate to every part of my body," Pam reported. "It was as if someone had poured very warm, thick oil over me and it was dripping all the way to my feet. Never had I experienced anything so phenomenal. My husband looked at me in astonishment and said, 'What's going on? You are all red!'

"'God is healing me,' I replied, pressing my hands to my face and then looking at them with amazement."

Within a few days the Lord gave Pam evidence of her healing. "All of my adult life I had experienced painful menstrual periods accompanied by heavy bleeding and clotting that lasted well over a week. This time, I passed one large clot, bled normally for three days, and was through.

"When the next month rolled around, I did not start at all. My home pregnancy test revealed the joyous reason: for the first time in my thirty-year life, I was pregnant!"

Nothing could quench the sense of euphoria Pam felt after waiting so long to receive this miraculous gift from God. But at the end of two weeks, she began running a fever of 102 degrees every afternoon. The doctor finally ordered her to the hospital for tests, which turned into a three-day nightmare. No one would tell her anything except, "We need more blood, dear," while inserting another needle in her arm.

On the third day the doctor reported that Pam had two viruses present in her blood: one could cause mononucleosis, and the other could cause birth defects or even death to the fetus if contracted early in a pregnancy.

"When he discharged me from the hospital with orders to

come to his office later that week, I entered into the darkest period of my life," Pam shared. "By the time I went back to the doctor I knew only one thing: God was not saying a word to me about my situation. All I could do was to continue walking in the last word he had given me, and that was a word of faith."

During the dark months that followed, Pam sought the Lord day and night for assurance that her baby would be all right. She wanted this more than anything. Finally, one morning during her quiet time, she felt the Lord speak to her through Job 13:15: "Though He slay me, yet will I trust Him" (NKJV).

"What a word!" she exclaimed. "I had been waiting for an indication that my baby was going to be born healthy and whole. But God was saying only that I had to trust him, even if he were to slay me."

Amazingly, that word was just what Pam needed in the days ahead. When she would awaken during the night with nightmares of physical deformities, that word gave her faith to get back to sleep. When the enemy tormented her with reminders of how she didn't deserve a healthy baby, that word sent him back into the hole where he belonged.

"Before long, I began to understand that because God had created *me* in the womb, he had the right to do whatever was necessary with my life as well as my baby's life," she said. "After all, it wasn't mine anyway. It was time for me to let go and trust him to shape it according to his plan.

"Meanwhile, back in the womb, someone was busy growing. By now we'd been hearing the healthy heartbeat of our baby for several months. I had successfully outgrown all but three maternity outfits. My November due date was one month away. Once again, God spoke to me when I least expected it."

Pam had begun to think she would live the rest of her life on the verse, "Though He slay me, yet will I trust Him." But one morning God interrupted her quiet time with Matthew 7:9: "Or what man is there of you, whom if his son ask bread, will he give him a stone?" (KJV).

She felt the Lord was telling her she would receive from his hand exactly what she had asked for: a healthy baby. Later that day, Chuck, not knowing of this incident, returned from a trip with a new record. "The Lord told me this song is for you," he said, handing the album to Pam and pointing to one of the titles. When she put it on the turntable the room was filled with the song, "If you ask him for bread, he won't give you a stone." It was her confirmation.

"That night, for the first time in seven months, I went to sleep *knowing* by faith that the baby in my womb was perfectly formed," Pam said.

Then two weeks before the due date, during a doctor's examination, she began to bleed profusely. He suspected *placenta previa* and sent her to the hospital for an emergency ultrasound. With her husband by her side, Pam waited in the darkened room and watched the ultrasound monitor. There on the screen was a perfect, thumb-sucking baby with the right-sized head and all the appendages intact. The doctor came into the room smiling and proclaimed that everything was fine.

"Two weeks later on November 3, 1984, Rebekah Faith was born, weighing nine pounds, one ounce," Pam smiled. "And throughout her life she has continued to be one of the healthiest children I know.

"Even if Rebekah had been born less than 'perfect,' it would not have changed the miraculous circumstances of her arrival here on earth. Nor would it have changed my conviction that 'though he slay me, yet will I trust him.' God is a Father who can be trusted to complete the perfection of his children."

Four years later Pam and Chuck buried identical twin boys within a week of each other. Even then, in the midst of her grief, she could still declare, without a trace of bitterness toward her heavenly Father: "Yet will I trust him."

Today, twelve years after her miraculous answer to prayer, Pam trusts him still. "We now have five healthy children full of promise," she said, "but we know only by God's grace and mercy can we complete the task of rearing them."

Unfulfilled Dreams

Many modern-day Hannahs have cried out to God asking for a child, but then have become fearful their dreams will never be realized. Beth, a special friend of ours, remembers that her painful journey began one summer during a time of spiritual dryness when she boldly prayed: "Lord, I need more of you if I am going to live wholeheartedly as a Christian. I need a major shift. Please intervene, Lord.... Do you hear me?"

She marked the moment in her mind, knowing she was truly in earnest. Then she waited for more of God. But God began to answer her in a way Beth did not at first recognize.

"Tom and I could hardly wait to have children," she shared. "We had recently bought a home and readied our lives for the little ones we dreamed of having. As months passed, a tragic truth began to reveal itself. We were unable to conceive."

Infertility most often unfolds slowly over the course of years. Couples keep hoping, waiting, fighting despair, enduring. But slowly the truth sinks in and the process of grieving begins. Beth says those who have not struggled with this problem, or walked with someone who has, may be quite unaware of the level of sorrow and pain that accompanies it. But the inability to bear children can be a significant loss—a very real grief—that leaves an indelible scar.

"We spent more than two years trying everything medically possible within our moral and ethical framework to conceive a child," Beth said. "Though fertility treatment is arduous, invasive, stressful, and expensive, we boarded that roller coaster of soaring hopes and deep disappointments. Still, at the end of all our efforts, we were unable to bring a child into the world."

When the treatments failed, Beth and her husband began earnestly seeking to adopt a child. Little did they know they had begun another two-year journey fraught with perils. Many opportunities to adopt came tantalizingly close, but each one failed. They would be minutes from holding their long-awaited child, only to learn one of the biological parents suddenly had a change of heart. The process began to seem like a very cruel trick they endured again and again as they questioned, "Where is God in all this?"

"In the midst of the years of struggle and stress, I spent a great deal of time 'in God's face,'" Beth told us. "I poured out my sadness to the Lord, calling upon him daily for help. I searched for meaning in these events, and dreamed of possible endings that could bring sense to this great struggle. I prayed on the doctor's table. I prayed when I could not sleep. I prayed in the car on the way to finalize an adoption, and on the way home through tears when it had failed. I prayed during the long, idle periods of waiting when no adoption was in sight.

"And finally, I learned to pray that if God did not plan to give us a child, would he please then give us more of himself to fill our emptiness."

God did not leave Beth alone in her pain, trying to hold on to his goodness. He gave her Tom, a stalwart, optimistic, loving husband. He gave her friends and family who assured her of God's loving care, his plan, and his work. They grieved with her, but kept pulling her up to the truths of who God is.

"Then the unimaginable happened," Beth reported. "I became pregnant! At the same time, a baby girl became available for adoption. But our agency did not want us to adopt if we were pregnant, so with regret we let this little one go.

"As the weeks turned into months, I began to heal from the sorrows of the past and embrace this most wonderful gift of life. I worried something bad might happen, but I told the Lord a miscarriage would be testing me beyond what I could endure. I entrusted him with this little life and let go of my fear."

With great excitement, Beth and Tom visited the doctor for the thirteenth-week ultrasound and anticipated seeing their baby. But as the doctor viewed the screen, his countenance clouded. He could not find a heartbeat. Gently he told them their baby had died. Beth's worst nightmare had become reality.

"At that moment I felt as if I'd been thrown from the jagged cliff of God's sovereignty," she said. "Now I was free-falling without any sense of where I would land. I was disoriented spiritually and emotionally. Devastated, confused, appalled, and outraged."

In those early days of grief, two passages of Scripture frequently came to Beth's mind. First, "Rachel weeping for her children and refusing to be comforted, because they are no more" (Mt 2:18). She now understood that kind of weeping. Beth also reflected on Isaiah 53, which speaks of Jesus as "a man of sorrows, and acquainted with grief" (v. 3, KJV). He was smitten, afflicted, bruised, and crushed.

"God allowed his Son to experience the deepest human sorrows and afflictions in order to draw near to us," she said. "It dawned on me that I was now in fellowship with his sufferings."

"God has a reputation for coming to men and women in the darkness of night," Beth mused. "He brought the children of Israel out of bondage at night ... called the child Samuel in the night ... announced Christ's birth to the shepherds at night ... opened the jail cell of Paul and Silas during the night. Darkness covered the earth when on the cross Jesus breathed his last and died for our sins. And God works in the darkness of our lives. It's where we should look for him."

The summer following her miscarriage, Beth vacillated between feeling as if God had carelessly crushed her under his foot, and feeling as if he had some incredible purpose that she could not yet see. She struggled between tremendous anger against God and a longing to trust him. Friends listened as she tried to make sense of the loss, and Tom loved her through the seemingly endless dark days.

"Bible study became like an anchor-stake driven into the ground for me," Beth said. "God's character and faithfulness, as depicted vividly in Scripture, encouraged me to consent to his timing and his ways—often so different from ours. So I waited."

Then on a cold January evening, the phone rang. It was the adoption agency.

"We had a son!" Beth exclaimed. "Jacob was waiting for us to come and take him home. We were overjoyed with the child God had given to us—this tiny, priceless gift. We have no doubt God had saved us for Jacob, and Jacob for us."

Despite their joy, Beth and Tom do not see the whole picture. They feel Jacob is only a piece of the story in God's larger plan for their lives, and God has not answered all their questions.

"His testing shaped our character and taught us endurance and hope," Beth said. "It allowed us to empty ourselves of our own notions and to bow before him—even when we felt sad and angry and did not understand. He simply has given us more of himself, which is exactly what I had prayed for in the beginning."

Painful Reality

Like Beth and Tom, most young couples who marry assume that some day, when they're ready, they will have children. But these days, increasingly, the inability to conceive becomes a painful reality.

The options are difficult and expensive, as Christy and Will, a couple who married in their thirties, discovered. After six years of marriage, with conception seeming more and more unlikely, they explored adoption possibilities.

"We were shocked to learn the enormous costs involved, but we went ahead with the necessary paperwork to have a home study done," Christy said. "Then Will took a military job and we moved to Germany, so we talked to an organization specializing in military adoptions. They told us there was a two-year waiting list, and by then Will would exceed their age limit."

Their only option was to put their desire in God's hands, so they asked the Lord to intervene if it was his will for them to have children. When they heard about a couple who had done a private adoption, they called the wife, Barbara, to get more information. She told them, "First, you have to find someone who's planning to give up their child for adoption. We really did it through prayer."

Christy left her phone number, and a few weeks later

Barbara called back with amazing news. A woman at a nearby military base had called her, needing advice. This woman's daughter, who had been living in the U.S., was now back in Germany with her parents because she was pregnant. She wanted to give up the baby for adoption. When Barbara told her about Christy and Will, the woman and her daughter, Gail, prayed about it and decided they were the ones the Lord had chosen.

"We were in awe as we watched the Lord work through all the arrangements," Christy told us. "One Friday in October Gail's mother called and said, 'You have a daughter and she wants her mommy.' Me, a mommy! After the final papers were signed we spent a day with Gail and got to know her better. We arranged to send her a Christmas card every year with a picture of Jennie."

Though Christy and Will had told the Lord they would be content with only one child if that were his will, a surprising call came from the States almost five years later. Gail was pregnant again, due in July. She wondered if they were interested in another child. And of course they said "Yes!"

Several months later an excited Christy flew to the U.S. to meet with lawyers and sign papers. She was present for the baby's birth, and was the first one to feed her son, Joel.

"I spent quite a bit of time with Gail," she reported. "She told me many of her friends had had abortions and urged her to do the same. It would have been the easy route. But even though she wasn't walking with the Lord, Gail knew abortion was wrong. We thank God she chose to give her babies life. The Lord had plans for Jennie and Joel all along."

Contented Without Children

Unfortunately, some couples' desire for a child never is satisfied—whether by birth or by adoption. Rosemarie told us that during their courtship days, she and her husband shared an enthusiasm about the prospect of having children someday. Imagine her shock when soon after the wedding he told her he didn't want to be a father, after all.

Rosemarie prayed he would change his mind, which eventually did happen. But after he finally became willing, she was unable to conceive. A series of tests revealed she was infertile, and her husband did not want to pursue adoption. Disappointed, she again had to deal with the prospect of never having children.

It wasn't easy, but over a period time, Rosemarie has reached a state of peace regarding the issue.

"I believe God has allowed this for the sake of the gospel," she says. "I'm able to spend hours in prayer as an intercessor. And because I don't have the responsibility of caring for children, I'm available to join prayer teams and mission outreaches on fairly short notice. The Lord has allowed me to go to Africa, Korea, and various parts of Latin America. I'm grateful I can serve him in this way."

How Can I Trust God?

Kim's story is another example of a couple who found that the matter of bearing children could become an emotional roller coaster. She and her husband Steve had been married four years when the exciting news of her first pregnancy was confirmed. The whole experience was fun for them. Feeling their baby kicking and moving in the womb and listening to his heartbeat at their doctor appointments was always thrilling. Throughout the pregnancy they were creating a beautiful nursery and buying baby things.

"But then I started having intense contractions too early and feeling pressure where I shouldn't have," Kim said. "We were almost eight months into the pregnancy, and knew it would be far better for me to carry the baby to full term. Our doctor examined me, thought everything seemed okay, and sent me to the hospital to be monitored.

"No one could have prepared me for the load that was about to come down. A nurse did an ultrasound to see what was happening. She never let on that she knew. The doctor came in. I really can't remember exactly what was said; I just remember the bullets. Birth defect. Spinal cord. Baby dying. No chance of survival. The words hit like bullets to my heart. We were completely devastated. The doctor explained to Steve that he needed to deliver the baby right away, as other complications were developing with me. Thirty-two hours of labor followed. I could not believe how much pain I went through—all for nothing."

Kim and Steve's son, Austin, was stillborn. They held him close and told him how much they loved him as their tears fell on his lifeless body. Then they left the hospital with empty arms to go home and plan a memorial service.

"I suppose my fog set in before the service, because most

of that week is a blur," Kim shared. "I don't remember much about it, except that there were very few supportive people who would hold us and let the tears flow. I couldn't stop the flood of emotion if I tried. I was so confused as I questioned, 'Why us? We wanted this baby. How? We had excellent pre-natal care. How can there be no explanation?'"

Kim's anger erupted, and fear and guilt prevailed. She wondered whether she could even survive as she and Steve faced the reality that most people in today's society simply don't acknowledge this type of loss. An unborn child who dies doesn't matter. Many didn't understand why they were grieving at all.

Young people in the twenty-something range don't often face such grief, nor bury children. Kim, not knowing how to grieve, thought the range of emotions she was experiencing must be abnormal.

"I felt horrible most of the time, but the few times when I did feel good, then I would be overwhelmed by guilt about it," she said. "The blender of my heart seemed to be on the puree cycle. Many people thought I should get pregnant again right away and the problem would be solved. Wanting to believe this, I was pregnant within eight months.

"But that pregnancy was terribly unfair to everyone in my life. Not only was I still very actively grieving for Austin, I had to watch my health and deal with all the 'extra baggage' the pregnancy brought. I did not want to build a nursery again after having painstakingly dismantled the last one. No, I didn't want to hear his heartbeat. No, I didn't want to know if it was a boy or a girl. Who cares, if it is just going to die anyway?"

Three times Kim was hospitalized for preterm labor. On Christmas Eve she cried and grieved so much for Austin that she went into labor again. She found it very difficult to love the new baby she was carrying; she didn't want to risk loving him for fear the cost would be too high.

Then one February night, the preterm labor could not be stopped. Spencer was born. Most parents' first question is, "Is it a boy or a girl?" Kim's was, "Is it alive?" She was relieved the terror was over. He was fine.

"I was thrilled, of course. Then I had to learn to love this little person I had tried so hard not to love. Our relationship was hard at first because this child could not truly 'replace' Austin, as I had thought he would. But now we have just celebrated Spencer's third birthday, and he has captured the love of everyone in his path. I especially love holding him at night.

Looking back on her tragedy, Kim counts many blessings he provided: A nurse who tenderly cared for them through a hideous labor and delivery experience. A pastor and his wife who guided them through a memorial service. A church that cared. She now leads workshops for other parents whose children have died.

Though she doesn't have all the answers, she can truthfully say, "I know how you feel...." To those grieving Kim says, "Meet yourself where you are. Don't put unrealistic expectations on yourself. It's okay to express your emotions in your own way, but do express them."

Embrace God's Plan

The biblical story of Hannah is an excellent example to all who grapple with this issue. After years of childlessness—and suffering persecution because of it—her prayer finally became, "If you give me a son, I will give him to the Lord for all the days of his life." Pastor Dutch Sheets says, "Hannah wanted a son, but God wanted a prophet.... When her prayer became aligned with God's will, he honored that prayer." Not only did God give her Samuel in response to her prayer, she later gave birth to five additional children.

How often we find that when we yield to God's ways and embrace his plan for our lives, his blessings far exceed our expectations!

Prayer

Heavenly Father, you see our empty cradle, and you see our great desire to have children. Your Word confirms that you truly are a Father to us, and we know you have a special love for children. Lord, we pray you will answer our hearts' cry for a child, whether by birth or by adoption. But we submit our wills to you, and trust your great plan and purpose for our lives. Please, Lord, cause your presence and your peace to sustain us as we wait upon you. In Jesus' name, Amen.

TEN

Crisis and Trauma

Let not your heart be troubled: ye believe in God, believe also in me.... And I will pray the Father, and he shall give you another Comforter, that he may abide with you for ever.

JOHN 14:1, 16, KJV

I did not go through pain and come out the other side; instead, I lived in it and found within that pain the grace to survive and eventually grow. I did not get over the loss of my loved ones; rather, I absorbed the loss into my life, like soil receives decaying matter, until it became a part of who I am. Sorrow took up permanent residence in my soul and enlarged it.... No matter how deep the pit into which I descend, I keep finding God there. He is not aloof from my suffering but draws near to me when I suffer.... The incarnation has left a permanent imprint on me. For three years now I have cried at every communion service.[1]

GERALD L. SITTSER

*W*hy do we see such tragedy in our world? Who can explain why disasters sometimes strike those who seem innocent and well-meaning? Those who deserve it the least?

A young mother killed by a drunken driver. A teenager paralyzed for life in a sports accident. A child who suffers brain damage because the delivering physician dropped him. Children killed in a terrorist attack. A missionary killed in a commercial plane crash because of pilot error.

Attempted explanations usually don't satisfy us. But author Elisabeth Elliot, whose husband, Jim, was tragically killed at age twenty-nine while on the mission field, says it's not necessarily wrong to ask the question "Why?" She writes, "There are those who insist that it is a very bad thing to question God. To them, 'why?' is a rude question. That depends, I believe, on whether it is an honest search, in faith, for his meaning, or whether it is a challenge of unbelief and rebellion. The psalmist often questioned God and so did Job. God did not answer the questions, but he answered the man—with the mystery of himself."[2]

A Fiery Nightmare

Belinda, the subject of the following story, could easily have asked "Why?" but she didn't. Let her tell the story:

"I fell in love with 'John' when I was nineteen, and a year later we were engaged. It should have been a very happy period in my life. But this man, like so many others close to me had done, eventually betrayed and hurt me very deeply. So I broke off the engagement.

"Two weeks later I was with a friend in a cafe one evening when John showed up and asked if he could take me home. I was still very hurt and angry toward him, but when he insisted, I reluctantly agreed to go with him.

"In the car silence hung in the air between us as John drove down the freeway. Then suddenly, he pulled over onto the shoulder near an on-ramp. Moments later a young man pulling onto the freeway fell asleep at the wheel, and his van rear-ended our car going fifty miles per hour, knocking our car forward almost forty feet. The point of impact was on the driver's side. I saw John go forward and hit his head on the windshield, then fall sideways toward me. He died instantly.

"I looked up and saw flames in front of me. Looking back, I saw flames behind me. The impact had cracked the gas tank and gasoline had splashed around the car, which was now engulfed in flames.

"I sat there thinking, 'This can't be real. This is a dream.... I'll wake up soon.'

"Of all the prayers I'd learned in church, the only one I felt touched God's heart was the 'Our Father'—so I began praying it over and over. Then I realized I was not waking up from this nightmare.

"Reality set in when I suddenly began to choke and gasp for air. The smoke was suffocating me! When I threw my hands in the air and started screaming, I realized a breeze was blowing above my fingertips. The plastic top of John's sports car had melted, making a way of escape for me. Standing on the door handle and the dashboard, I climbed out and jumped down, landing on my feet.

"I heard a man yell 'Stop, don't run!' and he hit me on the back with his jacket. My back was on fire and he was beating out the flames. Soon the LifeFlight helicopter was airlifting me to the hospital.

"The doctors told my mother the next three days were critical. Chances of survival were fifty-fifty. My mother says I almost died three times because of the smoke in my lungs. They would stick a tube down my throat and black soot would come out.

"While lying alone in my hospital bed one evening, I looked toward the door and saw a man in a long, flowing white robe with shoulder-length hair coming toward me. As he neared, I realized it was Jesus. And he was accompanied by a host of angels.

"In church I had always seen Jesus hanging on a cross. I believed he was the Son of God and that he died on the cross, but that was all I knew. The reality of his resurrection had never hit me until this moment. Here he was right in front of me. Alive.

"In my vision, Jesus sat on my bed and asked me to repent of my sins. He named some specific sins; I repented and promised I wouldn't do those things anymore. It seemed he knew everything about me. There was a gentle, understanding way about him, yet I sensed his authority and majesty at the same time.

"Then he spoke to me, 'Now you are reborn.' The moment he spoke those words, I felt life enter from the soles of my feet and go through me to the top of my head. I lay there repeating to myself, 'I'm going to live. I'm going to live.' I felt as if I'd been transferred out of darkness into his marvelous light of life!

"I felt so washed and cleansed that a childlike innocence was restored in me. Where there had been anger, bitterness, hate, and unforgiveness in my heart, now there was love, compassion, forgiveness, joy, and peace. His grace sustained me through the healing process over the months that followed, with burns covering 68 percent of my body.

"One evening in January the doctors told me they would have to amputate my fingers to prevent infection from setting in. Unless I agreed, they might later have to amputate my hand and maybe part of my arm. What choice did I have? I gave my consent. 'I'll never be able to do anything for myself again,' I cried over and over. Never to hold a comb or use a pen to write.

"Months of physical pain followed, with too many surgeries to count. Every day my wounds had to be washed and bandaged to prevent infection. Morphine injections didn't do much to ease the pain of this procedure. It felt as if the nurse was using a steel scrubber on my skin, not a soft washcloth.

"Many weeks after the accident, when I glimpsed myself in a mirror for the first time as an aide helped me to the bathroom, I gasped and almost fainted. She said, 'Now, Belinda, if you had seen yourself three months ago, you would know you look better now.' Four months after the accident, I moved from the hospital to a rehab center to relearn how to do the everyday things I had always taken for granted. It was hard and painful.

"I was asked to talk with a psychiatrist—even though I didn't want to. But I shared how my faith in Jesus was the reason for my joy and peace, and that I was looking forward to getting on with my life. She wrote in my chart that I was running away from my problems and not accepting what had happened to me.

"I never spoke to that psychiatrist again. Most people, like that doctor, expected me to be suicidal or angry about what had happened. Even today, with the burn scars so visible, many people assume the same thing.

"I'll never know why John pulled over to the side of the road that night, but I never blamed God for what happened; I am just grateful that Jesus came to me in such a beautiful way to give me life.

"Now, seventeen years later, as I look back, I marvel at God's love and faithfulness, which have helped me overcome the obstacles in my life. As for my physical needs, I've relearned how to do everything for myself—eat, type, bathe, dress, drive. I live a normal life. I still bear the physical scars of that tragic night, but the emotional and inner scars have been totally healed."

Today Belinda often has opportunities to speak to women's groups about her victory through tragedy. She also serves on a board of a Christian women's ministry.

Lost at Sea

Dot, like Belinda, has known great tragedy. She tells her story:

"The day after Thanksgiving in 1984, in the late afternoon, my son Jeff came over to my mother's and called me to come out into the yard.

"'Mother, this morning the Coast Guard picked up an SOS from Dad and David's boat,' he said. 'It said "Mayday, Mayday ..." then went off the air with a crackle. They said there was a bad storm in the Gulf last night....'

"My knees buckled and my body became numb. Spontaneous prayer gushed from deep within me as I began to groan. It seemed my spirit, soul, and body were about to disintegrate, but the Spirit of the living God held me together.

"Elbert, my husband of thirty-eight years, and my youngest son, David, twenty-five, were captain and engineer on this ninety-seven-foot vessel—one of several in the fleet of a new business harvesting crab in the Gulf of Mexico. They had a crew of four men aboard. Now they had disappeared. Gordon, my oldest son, was captain on the largest vessel in the fleet. Had not he and his wife come home for Thanksgiving, Gordon also would have been at sea.

"As the news traveled via radio and newspapers, multitudes of people we had known in ministries around the world began to call, write, and come to my side. They were special encouragers God sent me with their prayers, help, finances, and food.

"The Coast Guard, the Air Force, the Marines, and Elbert's company all searched for the missing boat. I searched. We got State Department clearance from Washington and permission from Cuba to search below the twentieth parallel. None of the teams could find any trace of the missing boat or its crew.

"Many nights I would go upstairs to my attic room and, with my cassette accompaniment tapes, sing and worship Jesus all night. Sometimes it seemed the agony of it all would make me lose my mind. But I would stuff my face in a pillow and scream, *Jesus, Jesus, Jesus!* Each time I screamed his name, peace and rest would come, pulling me back together.

"For a year I had no income. Several of my children and grandchildren came to stay with me—at one time there were eight of them under my roof. As a family we clung together, prayed together, searched together, waited together, went through everything together.

"Late that summer I experienced a personal breakthrough when, while sitting in my car one day, I began to weep with great compassion and forgiveness toward the man who owned the boat. Somehow I knew I needed to forgive him, though I'm not sure I understood exactly what I held in my heart—anger, perhaps. But with that prayer of forgiveness came my release.

"By August 1985, nothing had been found, and lawyers were still negotiating on the case. The disappointment and pressure of it seemed overwhelming. Finally, following their eight-month investigation, the boat company and the Coast Guard sent a letter of 'presumption of death' to my attorney, stating, 'All hands on board are presumed dead.' This was the document needed to submit to the insurance company. Exactly one year to the day after the boat disappeared, the case was settled.

"We were able to get a satisfactory settlement to take care of my financial needs and bring closure to the tragedy. 'Truly God has provided for you,' my attorney told me."

A Last Good-bye

When adversity strikes, can you still trust God to see you through your tough time? Marge and Ken experienced one of the most tragic losses any parent could imagine. Yet today, twenty-five years later, they will tell you they have known first-hand God's faithfulness—even when they lost their three children in one heart-shattering blow. Marge shares their story.

"Dusk was fast approaching, and I knew our three children and their friend Lydia had a long drive ahead of them after the weekend at our vacation cottage. We wanted them to leave sooner than we did so Lydia's mom wouldn't worry. I said, 'Gary, drop Lydia off, then go on home. We'll stop in town for church, but will see you later tonight.'

"I leaned in and kissed them—something I didn't usually do. Not when we'd be seeing them again in a few hours. But somehow it seemed important.

"Gary, seventeen, a high school senior, was behind the wheel. Callie, fifteen, sat beside him petting our dog, Poochie. In the backseat, eleven-year-old Diane chattered away with her classmate, Lydia.

"When they were out of sight, I walked back down to the cottage. Nothing foreboding hung in the crisp October air that Sunday night.

"I got busy locking windows, picking up books—and thanking God for such a delightful Sunday together. We'd shared Communion in a little church we'd visited that morning. The day had been so perfect. How quickly the time had slipped away!

"I finished my chores and joined Ken in the waiting car. But we'd been under way no more than fifteen minutes when bright flares warned of a roadblock ahead.

"'I think we'd better stop,' Ken said, reaching across for my hand. He called out to the state trooper rerouting traffic, 'Has there been a wreck? Anyone hurt?'

"'Yes. Four,' the man replied. Ken quickly pulled to the side of the road and stopped a pedestrian who had passed the accident scene. We learned from him that a truck coming from Baton Rouge had strayed onto the shoulder of the road. In trying to straighten his truck, he swerved too far to the left and smashed head-on into an oncoming car. He mentioned that a gold-colored compact car had been totaled.

"*Oh, my God*, I thought, realizing it could be our car. We ran frantically toward the wreck. Even though the front of the car was horribly smashed, we knew instantly it was ours.

"Then we saw them. Our three children and Lydia, lying motionless in the twisted metal. Gary was leaning over, as though trying to retrieve something from the floorboard. Callie's long brown hair covered her face. Diane and Lydia were still in the backseat, leaning against each other as though in a deep sleep.

"I screamed. My mind refused to accept what my eyes told me was true. I touched each one gently. My babies. Lifeless. This had to be a nightmare. Surely they were merely unconscious. 'Wake up, kids,' I pleaded. 'Please wake up.'

"Between great heaving sobs, Ken yelled, 'Why doesn't someone do something? Get a doctor. Send for an ambulance. Help us!'

"I clung helplessly to Ken. Then together we began to repeat one word: 'Jesus. Jesus. Jesus.' That weekend we'd been singing a song about the wonderful name of Jesus. Now his name was the only word we could utter, the only word that brought comfort.

"Someone led us to a house with a phone. Ken called our pastor at the church, who had already started the evening service. Through tears, Ken told him of our unbelievable tragedy and asked him to notify Lydia's mother.

"Our pastor dismissed the service so he could join us, but the congregation remained at the church to pray for us. While waiting for our pastor, Ken and I wanted to be alone. We went into a bedroom in the house where we were waiting and found, of all things, a small kneeling bench. We knelt together.

"'God, we can't handle this problem without your help,' Ken cried. 'Dear Jesus, this is greater than we can bear. Please bear it for us.'

"As Ken prayed, I was surprised by the memories which began popping into my mind, though my senses were numb.

Earlier in the summer Gary had been angry and blaming God because he had to pay a hundred dollars toward repairs on his car after a minor accident that wasn't his fault. After I gently encouraged him to give the problem to God, he prayed about it and told me he knew God would help him earn the money. Then the next day he found out the insurance would cover all the repair costs after all.

"'Wow, isn't God good?' Gary had said with a big grin. Tears splattered down my face as I relived that moment.

"I thought of Callie, who had fulfilled her heart's desire teaching young children about the love of Jesus in neighborhood Bible clubs that summer. And I remembered Diane, definitely our tomboy, who had helped her swim team bring home a trophy.

"Then, strangely, I thought of my mother. I could almost hear her telling me, '*Marge, God always prepares us for the valleys and provides his strength to see us through them.*' She'd been left with seven children to raise when Daddy died. Though I was only three at the time, I knew her inner strength had come from her strong Christian faith—and now it rose up in me.

"Within an hour, several close friends came to be with us. They went to identify the bodies of our children, sparing us that awful pain. They said it appeared all three had died instantly. Another couple took us home with them for the night, but we couldn't sleep.

"At the funeral home the next evening, more than fifteen hundred people came to pay their respects. I was so saturated with God's strength, I ended up comforting some who had come to comfort me. My constant awareness of his presence was like a warm peace radiating from my body to all I touched.

"I'd be lying if I said the following days weren't lonely. They were. But friends who came by to take me shopping, out to eat, or just to talk eased the ache.

"Then I began going through my children's belongings. Every little treasure I unearthed was like a gold nugget now aglow with new meaning.

"It became clear that for months God had been preparing us step by step for this triple loss. He'd led us to spend time together at the cottage, to enjoy weekends loving one another, to share our faith as a family. Looking back, I could see how God used the children's young lives to bless others.

"A high school girl Gary had dated and witnessed to about the Lord became a missionary. A little boy Callie taught in neighborhood Bible study became a campus youth leader. Even a sixth-grader from Diane's class became a Christian because, she said, she'd watched Diane's actions.

"Two years after our children's deaths, God blessed us with a baby we named Scott Allen.

"Surprisingly, the greatest victory from our triple loss is that we are privileged to comfort others who also have lost loved ones."[3]

Being Prepared for Crisis

Coping with a progressive illness can be traumatic—especially when you don't know what is wrong, as Judy can tell you.

She started out suffering intense headaches, dizziness, and pressure in the back of her neck. For six months she struggled to keep up with her public relations job, then she began experiencing a slowness when she walked.

Aware that something was desperately wrong in her body, Judy and her husband, Jerry, went away to the mountains for three days of prayer and fasting. Judy said she confessed any sin she felt separated her from God's best, then asked the Lord to help her order her priorities as she faced this crisis.

Finally, tests revealed a large tumor in her brain. "It must come out immediately," the doctor told them. Right away Jerry and her prayer partner began calling people across the country to pray.

After surgeons removed a piece of her skull and a tumor the size of a tennis ball, Judy awakened in the recovery room from a dream that she was in a prayer meeting. She wept when she realized the surgery was over and she could still think, feel, and respond to stimuli. She asked the nurse to play a cassette of praise music, and she worshiped the Lord as "Behold the Lamb" played. It was the beginning of her remarkable recovery.

During the next four days as she listened to tapes of Scripture verses on healing, Judy felt the Word of God literally was restoring her. The doctor released her with orders to remain quiet at home—no talking, no visitors.

"I didn't sleep for five days, but I rested in the Lord and meditated on his Word," she said. "I regained my strength much sooner than the doctors expected, but I never went back to my old job. Since praying about my priorities, I feel the Lord has called me to a more active role as an intercessor, and in missions."

Eight weeks after surgery Judy left for a missions trip to Africa, followed by trips to Korea and Israel. Many times she has crisscrossed the United States as an intercessor and prayer coordinator for several ministries.

How did she make it through such a serious surgery without panic? Judy is confident those days of prayer and fasting prepared her spiritually, even though the Lord didn't reveal the extent of the ordeal she was about to face.

"I learned I must always be prepared to meet God," she said. "I simply trusted him—and whether I lived or died I was in God's hands."

Faith for Any Crisis

Today some parents are finding themselves caretakers of their grandchildren as they face crises within their own families. Sally shares her story about how she and her husband Frank learned a new depth of prayer through such a challenge.

"Soon after Frank miraculously recovered from a serious heart attack, our teenage son and his pregnant girlfriend got married. A few months later our grandson Ronnie was born, perfectly healthy. But the marriage soon failed. Ronnie's mother really didn't want to be tied down with a baby, so my husband and I assumed the care of our new grandson.

"When he was five months old, Ronnie had a horrible reaction to a DPT shot and suffered heart damage. He was hospitalized for sixteen days. His heartbeat was so fast the machine couldn't record the rate, and his heart was greatly enlarged.

"When we brought him home we were told to expect one of these possible outcomes for his future: (1) he might die; (2) he might survive but be extremely limited in his activities; or (3) there was a slight chance he could outgrow his condition.

"About six weeks later we took Ronnie to a meeting where the minister prayed for God to heal him. We hoped for a good medical report when we took him for a checkup three months later, but he was no better. Six months after that he was only a little better. We kept saturating him with prayer. Thereafter, each time we took him back to the doctor he had improved. We kept praying and believing God for his total healing.

"Finally after six years of checkups, the cardiologist dismissed Ronnie, giving him the go-ahead to do whatever he wanted to do physically. He has since played baseball, football, and basketball.

"We know God spared our grandson's life for a reason, and he spared my husband's life so Ronnie—whom we legally adopted when he was still a baby—would have a dad and grow up in a stable Christian home. Ronnie is now fourteen years old, and the Lord gives us strength and wisdom for the task of raising a teenager."

The women in these stories, even in the midst of intense human anguish, experienced God's "divine dwelling place," as Hannah Whitall Smith calls it. She writes, "The last and greatest lesson that the soul has to learn is the fact that God, and God alone, is enough for all its needs. This is the lesson that all His dealings with us are meant to teach; and this is the crowning discovery of our whole Christian life. God is enough!"[4]

Yes, it's possible to experience God's divine dwelling place even here on earth, as we draw from him the strength needed to get through times of crisis or trauma. He is our fortress, our refuge, and our comforter.

Prayer

Lord, my mind is bombarded with questions about the trauma in my life right now. Nothing seems to make any sense—and finding answers that satisfy may not be possible. But Lord, I'm asking you to give me your peace and comfort in the midst of this trauma.

You've promised that we can cast all our anxiety upon you, because you care about what happens to us (1 Pt 5:7). Father, help me to hand over to you all my questions and worries about this situation. I choose to trust you no matter what happens, and I thank you for your faithfulness. Amen.

ELEVEN

Reaching Out to the Hurting

God has given each of you some special abilities; be sure to use them to help each other, passing on to others God's many kinds of blessings.

1 PETER 4:10, TLB

I retain a clear memory from childhood of the monthly charity of my Aunt Eunice. She would keep a little book from the Aged Pilgrim, Friend Society and visit women from that list every month without fail. Often I would accompany her as she took money or food or clothing or Christmas packages to those elderly women. In her own quiet, unglamorous way, Aunt Eunice taught me how to turn impersonal, chronic pain into a personal experience of sharing. She insisted on visiting the women, not mailing them packages, and she kept up her simple ministrations faithfully for years.[1]

DR. PAUL BRAND

*H*ave you noticed that after going through tough times yourself, you have more empathy for those dealing with a similar plight? Tough times tend to beget compassion for others.

One way we can reach out to the hurting is to practice the reciprocal commands in the Bible. We find more than fifty "one anothers" in the New Testament. These are just a few:

- Pray for one another.... James 5:16.

- Love one another.... John 13:34-35; Romans 13:8; 1 John 3:23.

- Accept one another.... Romans 15:7.

- Be hospitable to one another.... 1 Peter 4:9.

- Be kind to one another.... 1 Thessalonians 5:15.

- Serve one another in love.... Galatians 5:13.

- Carry one another's burdens.... Galatians 6:2.

- Agree with one another.... 1 Corinthians 1:10.

- Confess your sins to one another.... James 5:16.

- Forgive one another.... Ephesians 4:32; Colossians 3:13.

- Stop passing judgment on one another.... Romans 14:3.

- Teach and admonish one another.... Colossians 3:16.

- Have concern for one another.... 1 Corinthians 12:25.

- Honor one another.... Romans 12:10.

- Encourage one another.... 1 Thessalonians 5:11; Hebrews 10:25.

Perhaps the best way to reach out to the hurting is simply to be there to encourage, comfort, or help. The Greek verb that sometimes is translated "encourage" and sometimes "exhort" comes from the same root as the noun translated "comforter" or "helper" in John 14:26—referring to the Holy Spirit.[2] Just as the Holy Spirit comes alongside to comfort us, so we can stand with a struggling sister to help and encourage her in the midst of a trial.

Examples of Comfort

Maybe you feel you're at a loss for ideas on how to comfort someone who is struggling. Here are but a few ways women dealing with tough times have experienced encouragement from caring friends:

"After my mother died at home, a nurse friend came to help rid the room of the stench of cancer. She also prayed with me as we cleaned and cried."

"When we had to be out of town for a few weeks, a friend regularly visited my mother-in-law in the nursing home so she wouldn't feel abandoned."

"When my son went to prison, a close friend came and sat with me and let me talk and cry."

"When my husband lost his job, friends left groceries on our doorstep without ringing the bell so we would not know who our benefactors were."

"When our daughter was going through a painful divorce,

another woman who had experienced a similar heartache called regularly to encourage her."

"When my husband was dying with cancer, a friend organized volunteer nurses to sit with him through the night. I could sleep without worry, knowing he had professional care."

"After we lost our baby, a friend gave us a lovely rosebush named "Cherish." Each spring, right around the date of my miscarriage, it blooms in delicate scarlet roses in the garden just outside our kitchen window—bringing immense comfort year after year."

Importance of Friends

How comforting friends can be when we're going through tough times. I (Quin) keep by my desk a small maypole made of different colored ribbons to remind me of my twelve closest friends. I feel joy and encouragement when I look at it and think of each cherished friend represented by her special color. All of them have coped with tough times.

Most of these friends don't live nearby anymore. And since we moved out west four years ago from the deep south, it's been harder to make really close friends. Now I'm in my "silver years"—caught up in grandmothering, writing, and traveling to speaking engagements. But I make a special effort to visit longtime friends when I'm anywhere near their city. I've also been praying for God to bring the right friends into my life here in my new surroundings. And he is.

"Our friends, especially our best friends, are buffers against stress," says Dr. Brenda Hunter in her book *In the Company of Women:*

> We need our friends as confidants, as support players, as guides in rearing our children, as companions. They accept us, affirm us, and understand what it means to be a woman. They hold us accountable; they help us grow. When we're married, they provide an undergirding support for our marriages, and when we're single, they are the people we go to for in-depth understanding. Usually our closest friends also share our spiritual journey.[3]

One of the greatest pleasures of friendship is the spiritual bond we find when we pray in agreement for one another. We urge you to ask the Lord to link you up with one or more prayer partners who will stand with you through your own tough times. And of course you will reciprocate when the need arises. Friends who will pray with you—pointing you back to God, the real burden-bearer—are invaluable.

Needed: Substitute Moms

Another "partnering opportunity" we have as Christian women is to be a substitute mom for a young mother. One of the toughest times in a woman's life is when she is mothering her young babies and toddlers. Many have shared with us their sense of aloneness in trying to meet their children's needs while missing out on adult contact and conversation. Most do not live near grandparents or extended family members.

"Older women tell us to enjoy this season of our children's lives, for it will pass too quickly—which we know is true," one mother told us. "But that response doesn't really offer practical solutions, nor comfort us."

Is there a way to reach out to these needy women? Yes. Just offer to be a friend. Numerous young mothers long to be nurtured and accepted, to be held accountable to a "substitute mom," and to grow to become all God wants them to be. But where are the spiritually mature women to influence them and help them develop their potential?

Renee, mother of six from Titusville, Florida, wrote us about her spiritual mentor, Mary Jo Looney, who served her breakfast on Tuesday mornings for ten years. Some days Renee took the children along with her; other days her mother-in-law kept them. She writes:

"God brought Mary Jo into my life when my third child was just a baby and I desperately needed the encouragement of an older woman. She became a spiritual mother to me. Some days when I was discouraged, she offered me hope. She has been to me 'Jesus with skin on.' When I would arrive at her doorstep tired and weary from the demands of motherhood, she provided refreshment to my body, soul, and spirit.

"She has helped me to focus on God's value system and what is really important in life. While some frowned at the announcement of my last three pregnancies, she always urged me to remember that each child is God's righteous seed to raise for his glory. I've become a better mother as a result of her godly influence.

"Her words of encouragement have made me a better wife. 'That husband of yours is a keeper,' she'd say, enabling me to love him unconditionally."

Eight years ago, God impressed Mary Jo to ask the next ten young women she encountered to come to supper at her house. Seven came, and shared their family stories. They giggled and found they were normal. They had such a good time together, three volunteered to host a potluck brunch to see if others would enjoy fellowship as much as they did.

Today thirty to forty young women still gather once a month so Mary Jo and several other older women can teach and encourage them. They also break up into smaller groups to pray for one another before they leave.

Some of the young women who come are new in the community and in need of a friend. Others have emotional or spiritual needs. Someone always is there who can identify with and pray about their concerns. New moms bring their babies soon after birth for the others to see, love, and pray over.

I (Quin) think back almost twenty-five years to when Mary Jo became *my* friend. She shared her "Busy Mama" recipes, encouraged me to begin teaching women's classes, and taught me and my daughters how to decorate on a shoe-string budget. She's still there for me across the telephone miles—a cheerleader I've greatly needed on some days.

Some women are blessed to have been mentored by their

own mothers, though that is increasingly rare these days. Joyce Wright, wife of noted author and counselor Norman Wright, suffered the heartbreaking blow of learning their infant son would never progress beyond the level of a two-year-old. Besides the support of her husband during Matthew's twenty-two years of life, she was helped by the model of her mother's faith. Joyce writes of her:

She has been a wonderful example of trusting God each day, standing on Scripture during her son's bout with cancer and early death. I was a young wife, spiritually immature, and had no experience with deep trouble. So watching my mother made a great impression on me. I saw God transform my brother's rebellious life, and I learned to look past the circumstances of illness and death to spiritual victory. I saw my mother hang in there through very trying times. I knew her way was the only way I could get through my own tremendous challenge.[4]

These instances of spiritual mentoring illustrate the principle the apostle Paul wrote about:

"Teach the older women to be reverent in the way they live.... Then they can train the younger women to love their husbands and children, to be self-controlled and pure, to be busy at home, to be kind" (Ti 2:3-5).

Prayers Instead of Advice

Sometimes the most valuable thing a spiritual mentor can do for us is simply to pray. Anna remembers the tough times she endured when she and her husband were young missionaries with two toddlers. Living far from home and friends, they struggled with adjusting to a foreign culture and language, to difficult coworkers, and to harsh, insect-ridden living conditions. When Anna learned she was pregnant again, she longed for someone who could offer comfort.

She and her husband loaded their toddlers in the car and drove eight hundred miles to the capital city to visit an older couple who had lived and worked in this land for many years. They poured out their hearts to their friends, releasing all their pent-up frustration. The older couple offered no specific advice. They simply said, "Let's pray together."

"Somewhere in the course of our all-evening prayer time, God filled me with his love and his Holy Spirit," Anna reported. "I awoke the next morning a new person, and from that day on, Scriptures began to leap off the page when I studied my Bible, and a new love for Jesus filled my being. In spite of my physical weakness in the ensuing months, God miraculously gave us a healthy baby girl. The work he began in the home of loving friends, and the infusion of God's Word to my spirit, literally carried me through that dark period in my life. I often pictured myself clinging to verses of Scripture like a drowning person clinging to a life raft, and would go to sleep quoting Scripture promises."

Anna and her family have been through many deep waters since that time, but God's Word continues to be their mainstay. She's established the habit of having a daily quiet time with the Lord, along with Christian music to lift her spirits and give her a sense of his presence.

"I've learned I can't run from my circumstances or bury my head and pretend trouble isn't there," she said. "I must squarely face what God allows in my life, acknowledging my need for Christian fellowship and encouragement. We all need family, friends, and a church family to help bear the burdens."

Beyond Our Borders

At the beginning of this chapter we cite the verse which tells us to use our special gifts to bless others (see 1 Pt 4:10). Of course we should not limit this only to friends and acquaintances. God wants us to be willing to reach beyond our borders—beyond cultural, racial, language, or class barriers.

Many times I (Quin) have flown to another country on a prayer journey or to speak to a women's group. But a few years ago I joined an outreach team of American women on a mission of mercy to Guatemala. We traveled inland by way of bus, boat, and flatbed truck, then hiked through coffee fields to reach a small Indian village.

There we distributed medicines, clothing, gospel literature, and love to these precious people, many living in one-room houses with dirt floors and tin roofs. Each team member paid her own expenses, and blessed the people with her unique gifting—whether teaching, nursing, crafting, or music.

Barriers melted as we shared our love with the village women, and received their love in return. As we stood in a little hut to pronounce blessings over a family and sing praises to God in three languages, the experience deeply impacted every one of us.

Perhaps you can't see yourself going on such a mission trip to a distant land. But each of us can reach across barriers to touch those in need without leaving our own city.

A certified teacher we know volunteers to tutor math and science for teenage boys at a resident program for troubled youth. This is despite dealing with her own disappointment over a daughter who rebelled against their family's Christian values. By reaching out to others in need, the mother reports, she worries less about her own problems. "I'm keeping my hands off my daughter's situation, and leaving her completely in God's hands," she said. "And that's the best place she can be."

Another acquaintance invited women from a poor section of town to her lovely home with a pool, providing them a place of refreshment, encouragement, and Bible study. Over time, she established a women's center in the inner city to minister to women's needs and help furnish job-training skills.

Eleanor Workman is a dear friend of mine (Ruthanne) who took an interest in the needs of children in Haiti.

Encouraging her Bible study group to pray and to help, she began raising funds and taking short mission trips to Haiti while still working in a government job.

Following her heart, she eventually left her job and established an orphanage in Haiti for receiving abandoned and unwanted infants. Today, more than twenty years later, she oversees two orphanages and two schools ministering to hundreds of abandoned and poverty-stricken children. But it all began with simply reaching out to help the needy.

One of my greatest joys has been to take groups of volunteers of many ages and occupations to assist in Eleanor's work—including my own mom, and my mother-in-law who took her last mission trip at age eighty-four. Besides what they do for the children and the Haitian workers, they have been inspired by Eleanor's example. And they've returned home with a new zeal to reach out to the hurting.

Praying for Others

One of the reciprocal commands—"pray for one another"— sometimes means getting involved with strangers. I (Quin) remember a day when my prayer partner Fran and I visited a critically ill woman whom we didn't know in a nearby military hospital. My son had called and asked me to go; her son was one of his roommates.

"She's dying of throat cancer and since Mick has accepted the Lord, he wants to be sure his mother knows Jesus too before she dies," he told me.

After Fran and I went into her hospital room, she told us she had not been to church in years. Then she said, "I've turned my back on God all these years.... It's just too late...."

"No, no, it isn't," we assured her. Then Fran led her in a prayer to ask God to forgive her and to accept Jesus as her Lord.

"Come live in my heart, Lord Jesus. I want to be yours," she whispered a prayer. After that, I went to see her several times, taking her a Bible and devotional helps. Soon she lost her voice and couldn't talk. Within a few weeks she died.

At the funeral home I met her son, Mick. "She accepted Jesus before she died—I heard her whispered prayer with my own ears," I told him. "She was so happy you've become a Christian."

I'd hardly finished telling Mick the good news when an older woman spoke up. "Forgive me for listening in, but I'm Mick's grandmother. I've prayed for forty years for my only daughter—my prodigal child—to come back to the Lord. She made it! She actually made it to heaven. Thank you, Lord. Thank you, Jesus."

I left the funeral home thanking God for the opportunity to be a part of the answer to the prayers of that elderly mom. God does want us to pray for one another—sometimes even strangers.[5]

"It is possible to give away and become richer! It is also possible to hold on too tightly and lose everything. Yes, the liberal man shall be rich! By watering others, he waters himself" (Prv 11:24-25, TLB).

Prayer

Lord, forgive me for being so focused on my own problems that I sometimes fail to reach out to others. I choose today to release my own needs into your loving hands. Help me to continue making this choice each day—I know your ways are perfect, and you are able to do exceedingly beyond what I could ask or think. I want to be a channel of blessing to others as the Holy Spirit pours your love through me. Lord, I'm willing to be your hands extended to those in need. Please show me the ones you want me to touch. In Jesus' name, Amen.

TWELVE

Standing Through the Storms

*The Lord has His way in the whirlwind and in the storm,
and the clouds are the dust of His feet.*

NAHUM 1:3, AMPLIFIED

I understand the buffeted days and the days of no small
tempest, when neither sun nor stars appear. And it is
good to pass through such days, for if we didn't we
could neither prove our God nor help others. If any
experience of ours helps to bring others to our Lord,
what does any buffeting matter?

But we are not meant to live in a perpetual stormy
sea. We are meant to pass through and find harbor and
so be at peace. Then we are free from occupation with
ourselves and our storms—free to help others.

I want to live in the light of the thought of His coming, His triumph—the end of this present darkness, the
glory of His seen Presence. This bathes the present in
radiance.[1]

AMY CARMICHAEL

*I*nevitably we will encounter storms in life. It is our response to them that reveals just how tough we really are.

Just as storms come in the physical world, we can be sure sometime along life's way, we will experience a "wintertime" of spiritual storms also.

Stranded in the Storm

I (Quin) remember a particular literal storm that came with little warning. In the midst of one of the worst blizzards ever to hit North Dakota, I saw women standing tough in the spirit through very trying times.

I had been the keynote speaker at a women's retreat held in a Bismarck hotel in April 1997, attended by about ninety women from surrounding farming communities. When the retreat ended after lunch on Saturday the storm had already begun, and those who lived nearby got on the road toward home.

But half the group who lived farther away had to stay when the transportation department closed the main highways. I was to fly back to Colorado that Saturday, and have only one day at home before heading off to Texas. Then the airport closed down, so I couldn't leave, either.

The blizzard kept coming. Blankets of snow whipped by heavy winds buried all the vehicles in the parking lot and blew in under the hotel entry door, creating snowdrifts in the lobby.

Some women who phoned home learned their husbands were out burying cattle that had frozen to death. Others reported floods had already reached the basements of their homes, and the water was still rising. A few husbands were upset because their wives weren't there to help in the crisis.

What could we do? Pray. Trust God. Sing praises to him. It kept snowing—snow that would later turn to torrential floods. People stranded in nearby motels hiked to our hotel for food, which quickly became scarce since no trucks could make deliveries. Most hotel employees couldn't get home, either.

When the sun peeked out Monday morning, I got a taxi to the airport, hoping to make it home. It was one of the most harrowing rides I've ever had, with the taxi sliding on icy roads all the way. The airport finally opened and I got back to Colorado with only two hours in which to go home, repack my suitcase with summer clothes, and hurry back to the airport to catch a plane for Texas and my next retreat.

But the women of North Dakota—especially those from Fargo—went home to one of the worst disasters in their state's history. Sharon, a builder's wife from Fargo, who had been stranded with us, sent this report:

"As we returned from the retreat in Bismarck we could not believe the amount of snow, standing water, and ice. The closer we got to Fargo, the worse was the destruction of downed power lines—huge poles snapped like toothpicks stood broken in several feet of ice and water. Towns and farms were without electricity for five to ten days.

"For miles and miles out in the country all you could see was water. It was the most helpless feeling I've ever experienced. My husband rented a payloader and hauled in sandbags and workers. Then we spent four days sandbagging our job sites and helping neighbors, only to return home late each evening to see news reports of total destruction and even fires in parts of Grand Forks, farther north. Some said it was like being in a war zone, but we knew God was in control.

"When we learned our subdivision would not be protected by the large earthen dike the city constructed to save parts of south Fargo, I prayed for mercy. It came. The increase in water levels they projected never got to us, so our damage was less than it otherwise would have been.

"Through it all, God was very close. I sometimes felt overwhelmed by the chaos of destruction, but never to the point of abandonment or despair. God's peace prevailed in the midst of the turmoil. The answers I prayed for didn't always come, but I learned in a deeper way the sovereignty of God. On our local secular radio station, for about a month, they ran one-minute clips of messages by local pastors—all very inspiring and encouraging. Many hearts were open to God's help, and in God's mercy, Fargo and Grand Forks never lost one life."

Storms in the Bible

In reviewing the different storms mentioned in the Bible, we discover valuable truths about how God responds to his children when they are in a tempest.

God may provide a refuge, as he did for Noah. God told Noah to build an ark for himself and his family to protect them from the storm of judgment that was coming (see Gn 7). Because he obeyed, Noah's family had a place of refuge when the storm hit. The account says God shut the door of the ark, and the only window he provided looked upward. Those inside could not see the devastation of the storm and the flood; they could only look heavenward.

The ark is a picture of Christ. When by faith we trust him for salvation through repentance, forgiveness, and baptism, he becomes our ark of safety against judgment. And as the people of North Dakota discovered, he also is our refuge in the midst of whatever storms life may bring.

Since I (Quin) lived in Florida most of my life, I can readily identify with a reader who wrote, "Long ago I prepared for the storms of life before the storm hit." Each year as hurricane season approached, our family prepared for big storms—even if one never came ashore. We made sure we had on hand radios, flashlights, blankets, water, canned goods, boards, and tape for the glass windows. And we kept our car full of gas.

When a storm threatened our area, weather forecasters gave adequate warning so we could evacuate by driving north or inland to safety. It always amazed me that some people refused to leave, thinking they could ride out a storm of winds more than one hundred miles an hour. Some even lost their lives by such foolish decisions.

One night we took shelter in a church miles from the hurricane, and slept under the pews, cozy in our blankets, listening as the wind and rain pelted our refuge. I thought a lot about Noah that night. And I thanked God for the ark of safety for my family in that church.

I can't say that I was always as well prepared for the spiritual storms that came my way, but over the years I did learn how to prepare for hurricanes.

God may send a storm to turn us around, as he did in the case of Jonah. Instead of going to Nineveh as God had instructed, this disobedient prophet boarded a ship headed in the opposite direction. When the storm caused Jonah to confess his disobedience to the ship's crew, they threw him overboard. He ended up in the belly of a huge fish, where he made the quality decision to obey God instead of going his own way (see Jon 1-2).

Our experiences may not be as dramatic as Jonah's, but God certainly can and will use stormy circumstances in our lives to grab our attention when we're headed in the wrong direction, or when we need an attitude adjustment.

Her Storm Raged

God used the stormy circumstances in Sylvia's life to turn her around. During a period when she had rebelled against her Christian upbringing, she got married because she was pregnant. She was only seventeen years old. Then six months after the baby's birth, she was devastated to learn she was pregnant again. By now her marriage was in trouble, and she discovered her husband, Hank, was addicted to alcohol and serious drugs, including cocaine. Over the next six years he left her numerous times. But all these problems caused Sylvia to run back to God.

Then they moved back to their hometown and Hank left again—but this time she gave him an ultimatum. Until he truly committed his life to the Lord, he could not come back to her.

"I felt like a failure," she remembers. "I had shouldered the blame for our bad marriage, and even his alcoholism. Finally I told him I was going to have a Christian husband—whether it was him or someone else the Lord would give me."

Sylvia filed for legal separation so he would have to help support her and her two boys. She kept praying Hank would come to the Lord—even when a pastor counseled her to divorce him because of infidelity. When Hank would ask if he could come back, her answer was the same: "Not until you let God change you." It only made him angry.

"I learned how to live on my own, which I'd never done before," she said. "I loved the peaceful home God had given me, and my sons were content. The separation went on for six years, and I reached a point where I didn't even want him back. I did date others during that time, which I shouldn't have done—even if they were Christians. It distracted me from God's purpose."

Then one day when Hank called, she surprised herself by inviting him to accompany her to a Christian concert that night. She was even more shocked when he accepted. As the concert ended, the guest musician issued an altar call. Hank ran down to the front to give his life to Jesus.

"After about a week of talking with him, I knew he was truly a changed man," Sylvia said. "I felt I had no choice but to obey God and let him move back into our home. It was one of the hardest things I ever had to do—and I was angry at God. But God continued his healing work in me—then when I found out I was pregnant with our third child, I was very excited."

Sylvia and her husband not only grew closer together, he grew closer to the Lord with several men mentoring him in the Christian faith. Then one day he dropped a bombshell:

God was calling him to go to Bible college and train to be a minister.

"I couldn't believe it—and once again I was angry at God," she said. "I felt the Lord allowed all this to happen without giving me a clue that he wanted me to be a minister's wife. I told God all the reasons why I'm not suitable for the job. But we sold our house and went to Bible college, and my husband graduated valedictorian of his class."

While Hank spent the following year in seminary, he and Sylvia served on a church staff—he as associate pastor and she as church secretary. A year later they discovered problems with the church and were abruptly fired—events that shook Sylvia's faith to the core. But in this storm they sought counseling, which led to deep healing from their old wounds.

"I didn't realize how many problems we were carrying around from the old lifestyle," she related. "But God truly has changed both of us. Our marriage is fantastic, and I feel I have the best husband. A bonus blessing is that our children have a heart after God. God is faithful!"

Hank is now pastoring a church he planted, and Sylvia is his best supporter. After all, she has witnessed God's power in the midst of their stormy marriage—taking a drug addict and making him a preacher of the gospel. And changing her heart and attitude in the process.

Jesus Can Still Our Storms

Jesus can still the storm, as he did for his disciples.

These twelve men were terrified by a sudden storm, and they were upset to find Jesus sleeping in the back of the boat.

From our vantage point, it's easy to criticize these disciples. But most of us have experienced a storm at some time or other in our lives when we felt God was taking no notice of our distress. Jesus simply awoke and commanded the storm to be still, while chiding his followers for their lack of faith (see Mt 8:23-27).

How we long sometimes to have Jesus stop the storms in our lives! As we walk with him we learn he doesn't always still the storm of outward circumstances. But when we fix our faith on him, he calms the storm within our own hearts and gives inner peace in the thick of the storm.

Jan found, after her husband of forty-five years was diagnosed with macular degeneration, God wanted to calm her inner storm, not change her outward circumstances. When her husband was declared legally blind and not allowed to drive, she had to assume all driving responsibilities. His dependence upon Jan is stressful for both of them.

"This was quite a blow for us, but the Lord is teaching us patience, patience, patience!" she said. "It's so easy to fall into an argument over something he thinks he sees. He'll insist there's a squirrel on the fence when it's actually a robin. Silly little things that can be so annoying. The Lord is teaching me to laugh at these crazies and not to get upset over trivial matters. I'm now the official chauffeur—but I always have lots of instructions from him as I drive. Help, Lord!

"I'm praying more about little things than ever before—such as his frustration at not being able to fix things like he's always done, because he can't see to get the screwdriver into the screw.

"Between my husband and my mother—who just turned ninety-two and is very forgetful—life is an adventure these days. I have to look to the Lord to help me change my attitude, and learn to walk in his peace. Our problems really aren't difficult when we look around at others' troubles, though. This experience is keeping me close to the Lord, where I always want to be."

He Sees Us Through the Storms

God can take us through the storm, as he did with Paul.

While sailing from Caesarea to Rome, the apostle Paul and his traveling companions encountered a ferocious storm. When hope of survival was almost gone, God sent an angel to comfort Paul (see Acts 27:23-24). Though he was a prisoner on board that ship, Paul was the one who received God's instructions on how they could come through the storm.

Two things were necessary: they had to reorder their priorities and throw overboard all excess baggage. Then Paul told the crew to cut the ropes to the lifeboats—they had to depend on God's plan, not their own solution. They lost the ship, but survived the storm.

Author William Gurnall suggests one reason God doesn't always deliver us from the storm as soon as we would like: it is to give our faith the opportunity to grow stronger. He uses the analogy of learning to walk:

When a mother is teaching her child to walk, she stands back a short distance and holds out her hands to the child, beckoning him to come. Now if she exercises her strength to go to her little one, the child is ill-served, for his unsteady legs are denied the practice they need. If she loves him, she will let him suffer a little at present to ensure his future health. Just so, because God loves His children, He sometimes lets them struggle to strengthen the legs of their unsteady faith.[2]

Peace in the Midst of the Storm

On May 5, 1995, the small Texas community where Rose and Grady live was hit with what was described as the worst hailstorm ever recorded in our nation. They lost seventeen windows, including storm windows; their carpet was ruined; their curtains were shredded; their roof was destroyed; and the lifetime-guaranteed vinyl on the upper story of their house was slivered.

Huge hailstones blew in through broken windows and piled up against the door of one room, making it impossible even to open the door. Their van was totaled and a truck and tractor badly damaged. Thankfully, another car was in the shop to be repaired at the time.

Rose and Grady took shelter in a bathroom. When the storm subsided and they looked out, the surrounding trees were stripped of their leaves and some of their bark.

"To look outside was like looking at a war zone," Rose reported. "Our scenery changed from springtime with multitudes of leaves, to wintertime with bare branches. Devastation was everywhere.

"I was amazed at the peace I felt on the inside in spite of the storm's destruction on the outside. And just as the Scripture says—everything did work together for good. We developed relationships with neighbors that we are so grateful for today. And I've been told many times that our home—since it has been repaired—is prettier than it ever had been. This time God didn't quiet the storm, but he brought us through it."

A Storm to Deliver Us

God may use the storm itself to deliver us, as he did with Moses.

When the Israelites fled from Egypt and came to the shore of the Red Sea, they had reached a virtual impasse. There was no way to cross the sea, and Pharaoh's army was in hot pursuit behind them. It's this historical event that inspired the expression "between the devil and the deep blue sea"—meaning there's simply no way out by natural means.

Moses told the people, "Do not be afraid. Stand firm and you will see the deliverance the Lord will bring you today. The Egyptians you see today you will never see again" (Ex 14:13).

When Moses stretched out his hand over the sea, God sent a windstorm—a strong east wind—which divided the waters. The next day the Israelites crossed over on dry ground, Pharaoh's chariots still following them. But after the Israelites had gone through, God instructed Moses to stretch out his hand over the sea again. When he did, the waters flowed together, and every single Egyptian was destroyed (see Ex 14:21-31).

Faith Can Grow in Storms

Many women like Annette, the woman in our next story, are still standing through the storms and trusting God for a resolution. In the midst of it, her faith is having an opportunity to grow.

When adult children make wrong marriage choices, parents often suffer with them through traumatic tough times and the grievous consequences. Annette, a mother whose daughter and grandchildren are now living with her to escape an abusive marriage, told us about her heartrending experience.

This trial began when the daughter Becky (not her real name) met and fell in love with an international student at a Christian Bible study group on a college campus.

"They convinced us they were meant for each other," Annette said. "Becky had visited his family and knew about the cultural differences, the fact she would have to learn another language, and live thousands of miles away from her own family. Though my husband felt strongly against the idea of this match, we didn't try to stop her. We were led to believe they would live overseas and work in a ministry there for a few years, then settle in the United States. But that never happened."

Several years passed, with Becky and her husband living in inadequate housing and working at jobs neither of them particularly liked. She struggled to learn the language and cope with the living conditions. But the greatest shock was realizing that in this culture, wives were expected to submit to the husband's wishes in everything. This practice had not been that evident during her short visit before the wedding.

Becky's husband expected her to hold a job, run the home, be available for all his needs, take care of their children, and never make more than a minimal purchase without his permission. She endured verbal abuse daily. Not only did he cut down her sense of self-worth, he told her everything she could or could not do.

Though he considered himself a committed Christian, he stopped going to church after a falling-out with some of the leaders a few years ago. Yet he continued to use Scripture as a weapon to control his wife.

By nature, Becky had always been reluctant to give up on any venture she undertook, so she kept trying to adjust, trying to please. But after enduring years of her husband's tyranny and explosive anger, she realized she was trapped in an abusive marriage that held little hope for change. The added responsibilities of caring for children only intensified the problems.

"Finally, although she'd been browbeaten until she barely could think for herself, she made a plan to leave," Annette said. "She was so terrified when she got to our house that a family member would have to stay in the same room with her until she fell asleep. She lived in fear that her husband would try to take her children away."

Annette and her husband realized they were in a fierce spiritual battle. "The enemy's schemes were clever and constant," she said. "But the Lord instructed us to set a guard over our mouths and not to respond to the accusations of Becky's husband against our daughter or our family. He could easily tongue-lash and berate someone in one instant, then moments later try to carry on a normal conversation with that person as though nothing unusual had happened. Our silence made him even more angry and frustrated."

Annette shared the prayer strategy she feels the Lord gave her family to use in this ongoing battle as they stand in their storm:

- To pray Psalms 35 and 91 for Becky and her children—for God's angels to watch over them.
- To constantly forgive Becky's husband, especially each time he sends a hateful or threatening letter. Walking in forgiveness keeps their hearts open to God's direction and blessing.
- To ask God to cancel the prayers of well-meaning people who are praying she will return to her husband despite his abuse.
- To pray Becky's husband will find repentance leading to the knowledge of truth, and that he will come to his senses and escape from the trap of the devil (see 2 Tm 2:26).
- To pray that Becky's children will have strong Christian influences, both through her family and through others God will cause to cross their paths.

The words of Nahum the prophet really are true: "The Lord has His way in the whirlwind and in the storm." (Na 1:3, AMPLIFIED).

If God is big enough to control the powerful forces of nature, we must believe he is big enough to resolve our stormy situation, and honor his promises. One of our prayer partners expresses the essence of the choice we all face:

Every woman has a point in time when she has to make a decision to believe that God can handle what she cannot handle. After coming to that place of trusting Jesus, I learned to stand on the Word when I couldn't see any light or hope in the natural.

We pray the next time you find yourself facing a storm, you will take courage from these biblical examples, and from the women in this book who have shared their stories.

Prayer

Lord, I come to you concerning the stormy situation I'm going through right now. I hang my hope, faith, and trust on your strong right arm reaching out to save. Steady me in this storm, and give me your peace. Help me to stand as an intercessor for those who are affected by this storm, and give me a prayer strategy for them until they come through safely. Just as you quieted the storm for your disciples who were so afraid, I pray you will quiet the storm in our lives. In Jesus' precious name I pray, Amen.

Epilogue

Betrayal.
Lost dreams.
Death of a friend.
Crushed expectations.
Disappointments too painful to share.

All of us have experienced some of these truly tough times. But now that I have reached my silver years, I can say unequivocally that each time I've walked through a painful, tough time, my relationship with God has grown stronger.

Why? Because he is the only one I can fully trust and depend upon. He is the reservoir of strength enabling me to get through.

The other day as I read these words from Romans 5:3-4a in my Amplified Bible they seemed to penetrate my heart: "Moreover—let us also be full of joy now! Let us exult and triumph in our troubles and rejoice in our sufferings, knowing that pressure and affliction and hardship produce patient and unswerving endurance. And endurance (fortitude) develops maturity of character (approved faith and tried integrity)."

Who would sign up for a course in pressure, affliction, hardship? Hardly anyone. But who among us would not want to be known for our endurance, maturity of character, faith, and integrity? Count me in.

Sometimes we think we just can't take any more hard times! We've reached our limit. When I feel that way I remind myself of a lesson I learned from my two-year-old grandson, Lyden Benjamin.

While walking with him from my house to his, it seemed we would never get to his front door because he stopped to smell the roses all along the way. In my impatience I wanted to get on with the journey, to reach our destination. But his pleasure at the beauty and fragrance of the flowers made his walk a delight.

I realized how I tend to hurry through life, not savoring my "golden moments" and the beauty of God's creation along the way. Tough times come, yes. But even if our path leads through suffering, we can find flowers along the way. And with the thorns of the rose is also the perfume.

How glad I am that this earth is not our final home. And that because of Jesus' death and resurrection we have the promise of eternal life with him.

I hope by now you have come to depend more and more on Jesus as your Savior. Because that's what will sustain you through life's tough times.

Quin Sherrer

Notes

ONE
Are You Going Through Tough Times?

1. Dr. Paul Brand and Philip Yancey, *In His Image* (Grand Rapids, Mich.: Zondervan, 1984), 291.
2. Roger C. Palms, *Bible Readings on Hope* (Minneapolis: World Wide Publications, 1995), 49.
3. Antoinette Bosco, *The Pummeled Heart* (Mystic, Conn.: Twenty-Third Publications, 1994), 16, 27.
4. Corrie ten Boom, *Not Good if Detached* (London: Christian Literature Crusade, 1957), 95–96.

TWO
When Hardship Hits Home

1. Catherine Marshall, from *A Closer Walk,* quoted in "The Breakthrough Intercessor" Newsletter (May/June 1997), 12.
2. Hannah Whitall Smith, *The God of All Comfort* (Chicago: Moody, 1956), 112.
3. Evelyn Christenson, *What Happens When Women Pray* (Wheaton, Ill.: SP Publications, 1975), 66–67.
4. Ray Beeson and Ranelda Mack Hunsicker, *The Hidden Price of Greatness* (Wheaton, Ill.: Tyndale, 1991), 87–88.
5. Dean Sherman, *Spiritual Warfare for Every Believer* (Seattle, Wash.: Frontline Communications, 1990), 140.

THREE
Healing Family Heartaches

1. T.D. Jakes, *Woman, Thou Art Loosed!* (Tulsa, Okla.: Albury, 1996), 59.

FOUR

Adversity in Marriage

1. Elisabeth Elliot, *Love Has a Price Tag* (Ann Arbor, Mich.: Servant, 1979), 108.
2. Paula Sandford, *Healing Women's Emotions* (Tulsa, Okla.: Victory House, 1992), 45, 61.
3. Excerpted from Elaine Keith, "How God Saved Our Marriage" *Aglow Magazine* (Lynnwood, Wash.: Aglow Publications, 1986), Spring, 15–21. Used with permission.
4. Laurie Hall, *An Affair of the Mind* (Colorado Springs: Focus on the Family, 1996), 98–99.
5. Hall, 231.
6. Hall, 239.

FIVE

Overcoming Betrayal and Divorce

1. From Chuck Swindoll's book *Simple Faith*, as quoted in Max Lucado, *Life Lessons Series; Books of Ruth and Esther* (Dallas: Word, 1996), 38.
2. Alfred Ells, *Restoring Innocence* (Nashville: Nelson, 1990), 210–11.
3. Carolyn A. Driver, "How to Walk With God When Your Spouse Doesn't," *Charisma Magazine* (Lake Mary, FL: Strang Communications, March 1997), 36.
4. Natalie R. Peterson, "Now's time to think Domestic Violence Prevention," *San Antonio Express-News* October 15, 1997, 5B.
5. Catherine Clark Kroeger and James R. Beck, *Women, Abuse, and the Bible* (Grand Rapids, Mich.: Baker, 1996), 20, 186.
6. Patricia Evans, *The Verbally Abusive Relationship* (Holbrook, Mass.: Media Corporation, 1996), 83-84.
7. Catherine Marshall, *Light in My Darkest Night* (Grand Rapids, Mich.: Chosen Books, Inc., a division of Baker Book House, © 1989 by Leonard E. LeSourd), 27.
8. Marshall, *Light in My Darkest Night,* 255.
9. Elisabeth Elliot, *Keep a Quiet Heart* (Ann Arbor, Mich.: Servant, 1995), 51.

SIX

Never Alone: Facing Widowhood

1. Ruth Sissom, *Instantly a Widow* (Grand Rapids, Mich.: Discovery House, 1990), 20.
2. Sandford, 39, 82.
3. Ruth Myers, *31 Days of Praise* (Sisters, Ore.: Multnomah Press, 1994), 127.
4. Sissom, 64.

SEVEN

Grief and Disappointment With God

1. Walter Wangerin, Jr., *Mourning into Dancing* (Grand Rapids, Mich.: Zondervan, 1992), 157.
2. Herman Riffel, *Learning to Hear God's Voice* (Old Tappan, N.J.: Fleming H. Revell [A Chosen Book], 1986), 116–17.

EIGHT

When You Pray for Healing

1. Excerpted from Mickie Winborn, *Through a Glass, Darkly* (Tulsa, Okla.: Harrison House, 1997).
2. Joni Eareckson Tada and Steven Estes, *When God Weeps* (Grand Rapids, Mich.: Zondervan, 1997), 117–118.
3. Quin Sherrer and Ruthanne Garlock, *A Woman's Guide to Spiritual Warfare* (Ann Arbor, Mich.: Servant, 1991), 26–28.

NINE

When the Cradle Is Empty

1. Philip Yancey, *Disappointment With God* (Grand Rapids, Mich.: Zondervan, 1988), 200–201.

TEN
Crisis and Trauma

1. Gerald L. Sittser, *A Grace Disguised: How the Soul Grows Through Loss* (Grand Rapids, Mich.: Zondervan, 1996), as quoted in a book review by Christopher A. Hall in *Christianity Today* (March 3, 1997), 46–47.
2. Elisabeth Elliot, *On Asking God Why* (Old Tappan, N.J.: Revell, 1989), 18.
3. Excerpted from "Our Triple Loss" by Marge DeZwaan, as told to Quin Sherrer, *Christian Life Magazine* (Lake Mary, Fla.: Strang Communications, May 1984), 35–43. Used by permission.
4. Smith, 241.

ELEVEN
Reaching Out to the Hurting

1. Dr. Paul Brand and Philip Yancey, *In His Image* (Grand Rapids, Mich.: Zondervan, 1984), 276.
2. *Strong's Exhaustive Concordance* (Grand Rapids, Mich.: Baker, 1984), references #3870 and #3875.
3. Brenda Hunter, *In the Company of Women* (Sisters, Ore.: Multnomah Books, 1994), 116.
4. Norm and Joyce Wright, *I'll Love You Forever* (Colorado Springs: Focus on the Family, 1993), 9.
5. Quin Sherrer and Ruthanne Garlock, *How to Pray for Your Family and Friends* (Ann Arbor, Mich.: Servant, 1990), 110–12.

TWELVE
Standing Through the Storms

1. Stuart and Brenda Blanch, *Learning of God: Readings from Amy Carmichael* (Fort Washington, Pa.: CLC, 1985), 129.
2. William Gurnall, *The Christian in Complete Armour,* Vol. 1, abridged ed. (Carlisle, Pa.: Banner of Truth Trust, 1986), 56.

Recommended Reading List

Bevere, John. *Breaking Intimidation: How to Overcome Fear*. Lake Mary, Fla.: Creation House, 1995.

Eareckson Tada, Joni and Steven Estes. *When God Weeps: Why Our Sufferings Matter to the Almighty*. Grand Rapids, Mich.: Zondervan, 1997.

Elliot, Elisabeth. *A Path Through Suffering: Discovering the Relationship Between God's Mercy and Our Pain*. Ann Arbor, Mich.: Servant, 1990.
_____. *On Asking God Why*. Old Tappan, N.J.: Revell, 1989.

Ells, Alfred. *Restoring Innocence*. Nashville: Nelson, 1990.

Hall, Laurie. *An Affair of the Mind*. Colorado Springs: Focus on the Family, 1996.

Hansen, Jane. *Inside a Woman*. Lynnwood, Wash.: Aglow Publications, 1992.
_____. *Fashioned for Intimacy*. Ventura, Calif.: Regal, 1997.

Jakes, T.D. *Woman, Thou Art Loosed!* Tulsa, Okla.: Albury, 1996.

Kinnaman, Gary. *My Companion Through Grief*. Ann Arbor, Mich.: Servant, 1996.

Kroeger, Catherine, and James Beck, eds. *Women, Abuse and the Bible: How Scripture Can Be Used to Hurt or Heal*. Grand Rapids, Mich.: Baker, 1996.

Marshall, Catherine. *Light in My Darkest Night*. Grand Rapids, Mich.: Baker, 1989.

Meir, Paul. *Don't Let Jerks Get the Best of You: Dealing with Difficult People*. Nashville: Nelson, 1993.

Minirth, Dr. Frank B., and Dr. Paul D. Meier. *Happiness Is a Choice. A Manual on the Symptoms, Causes, and Cures of Depression*. Grand Rapids, Mich.: Baker, 1988.

Mitsch, Raymond R. and Lynn Brookside. *Grieving the Loss of Someone You Love.* Ann Arbor, Mich.: Servant, 1993.

Oliver, Dr. Gary J., and Dr. H. Norman Wright. *Good Women Get Angry: A Woman's Guide to Handling Anger, Depression, Anxiety and Stress.* Ann Arbor, Mich.: Servant, 1995.

Sandford, Paula. *Healing Victims of Sexual Abuse.* Tulsa, Okla.: Victory House, 1988.
_____. *Healing Women's Emotions.* Tulsa, Okla.: Victory House, 1992.

Sheets, Dutch. *Intercessory Prayer.* Ventura, Calif.: Regal, 1996.

Sherrer, Quin, and Ruthanne Garlock. *A Woman's Guide to Breaking Bondages (Breaking Free From Strongholds).* Ann Arbor, Mich.: Servant, 1994.
_____. *A Woman's Guide to Spirit-Filled Living.* Ann Arbor, Mich.: Servant, 1996.
_____. *A Woman's Guide to Spiritual Warfare.* Ann Arbor, Mich.: Servant, 1991.
_____. *How to Pray for Your Children.* Revised edition. Ventura, Calif.: Regal, 1998.

Sherrer, Quin. *Miracles Happen When You Pray (True Stories of the Remarkable Power of Prayer).* Grand Rapids, Mich.: Zondervan, 1997.

Sissom, Ruth. *Instantly a Widow.* Grand Rapids, Mich.: Discovery House, 1990.

Yancey, Philip. *Disappointment With God.* Grand Rapids, Mich.: Zondervan, 1988.